S0-EHD-929

Graham Greene

AN EXISTENTIAL APPROACH

GRAHAM GREENE

AN EXISTENTIAL APPROACH

GANGESHWAR RAI

Associated Publishing House
New Delhi-110005

Associated Publishing House
New Market, Karol Bagh, New Delhi-110005

PRINTED IN INDIA

PRINTED AND PUBLISHED BY R. K. PAUL FOR ASSOCIATED PUBLISHING HOUSE, NEW DELHI-110005

Preface

THE imaginative works of Graham Greene, who is one of the most significant novelists of our age, have their starting point in the twentieth-century breakdown of traditional values. His reaction to this breakdown is seen in his choice of man's alienation as his central theme. I was attracted to Greene for his deep awareness of the plight of the contemporary man and his emphasis on the importance of existential values. Greene is one of those writers who represent a significant phase of the twentieth-century mind notable for its rejection of worn-out ideals and its unflagging attempts at building up a new morality.

I have attempted to study Greene's important novels, plays and short stories from the existential point of view. Greene has usually been seen by his critics as a religious writer or as a writer with certain thematic obsessions. K. Allott and M. Farris insist on Greene's preoccupation with the idea of corrupted childhood leading to a predilection for horror and violence in later life. They define Greene's canon in terms of "obsession". According to them, the terror of life and its origin in the early years is Greene's central theme.[1] Mesnet discusses Greene's tragic vision of man's predicament, the fatality of evil and the power of grace—the two forces at war within him.[2] John Atkins's criticism is mainly biographical,[3] and David Pryce-Jones has produced a study of a religious man.[4] A. A. DeVitis discusses Greene as a writer preoccupied with religious themes.[5] Kunkel explains Greene's use of religious subject-matter, traces characters and themes, analyses situations, symbols and evaluates literary and religious influences on Greene's maturing art.[6] Only a few stray articles dealing with Greene's treatment of certain existential issues have appeared in periodicals. J. Noxon discusses *A Burnt-out Case* with reference to Kierkegaard's stages on life's way,[7] Lucio P. Routolo discusses Rose as an absurd heroine[8] and R.O. Evans points out the similarity between the thoughts of Greene and Sartre in Greene's *The Quiet American*.[9] Some critics have made passing comments on Greene as an existentialist. For instance, Hazel E. Barnes discovers in his works "off moments of near existentialism",[10] Marcel, the Catholic existentialist, did claim Greene "as one of them".[11] To R.O. Evans,

"Greene's variety of existentialism is essentially Catholic"[12] and R.W.B. Lewis thinks that "Greene plainly, even self-consciously, belongs to that particular strain of the Christian tradition now reanimating itself in its controversy with the atheistic existentialism".[13] But there is no full-length study in English dealing with the existential note present in Greene's writings.[14] This justifies the attempt that the present book makes.

Existentialism is fundamentally an attitude, a way of perceiving the man and the world. As such it has existed ever since man confronted his own frailty and the meaninglessness of existence. One may trace its origin in Greek philosophy and even in the Bible. But as a regular philosophy it became popular after the two World Wars, which gave a shock to the facile doctrine of progress appealing to the nineteenth-century mind. It is, in fact, a comprehensive philosophy embracing the atheism of Sartre, the Protestantism of Kierkegaard, the Roman Catholicism of Marcel and Judaism of Buber. But the existential philosophers are divided into two groups, Christian and atheistic, which have been dealt with at some length in the second and third chapters of this monograph. As existentialism has been interpreted variously, it is not easy to determine the common ground. Some hail it as a return of the religious element into a world overridden by materialism. The others denounce it as the expression of despair and irrationalism and a disastrous surrender to nihilism. In very general terms, existentialism may be described as an attempt to reach the inmost core of human existence in a concrete and individual manner. It lays stress on the significance of individual freedom which leads to faith in God in the case of religious existentialists and to faith in man in the case of atheistic existentialists. A keen recognition of his inability to run life all by himself, *i.e.*, "sickness unto death" leads man towards readiness for faith in God. Atheistic existentialism, of which Sartre is the best representative, declares that if God does not exist, there is at least one being whose existence comes before its essence, a being which exists before it can be defined. That being is man or, as Heidegger has it, the human reality. Thus existentialism has produced the most penetrating form of Christian faith as well as the most nihilistic type of human self-assertion. It emphasizes the character of the existential man and the importance of existential humanity. The existential man is someone who lives in sincerity to his own self independent of the accepted norms of behaviour. He has the courage to stare unafraid at emptiness, tragedy and death. Existential humanity is man's pure love for man which arises from his direct personal and emotional experience and which is not derived from a source outside himself. Thus existentialism may be viewed as an effort to reinstate human personality in the face of dehumanization brought about by our industrial and technological culture. This is a task which conventional religion no longer appears capable of performing. In giving man his absolute freedom existentialism may appear to crown him in a desert and make him the sovereign of an empire of nothingness. But this nothingness is the ground of human existence, of human responsibility and of human action. For man is nothing else but that which he makes of himself.

Graham Greene admits having read "Kierkegaard"[15] whose existential thoughts must have influenced him. The existential influence might also have percolated into his writings as a result of the ideas that were in the air in the early twentieth century. But the main source of his existential themes seems to lie in his own experience. The existential issues which appear in Greene's writings flow from his personal vision. He explores his own self and tries to realize what he finds there in his work. The Introduction of this book brings out the affinity between the existential themes of Greene and his private phantasy. The chapter dealing with the three early novels – *The Man Within*, *It's a Battlefield* and *England Made Me*—shows Greene's concern with the exploration and discovery of man's isolation. The protagonists of these novels are sad, solitary figures who have done with society and all gainful activity and suffer from a sense of alienation resulting from contemporary chaos as well as their own dispositions. The chapters on religious novels (*Brighton Rock*, *The Power and the Glory*, *The Heart of the Matter*, *The End of the Affair* and *A Burnt-out Case*) and his plays (*The Living Room*, *The Potting Shed*, *The Complaisant Lover* and *Carving a Statue*) raise the problem of existential faith and point out Greene's attraction towards the anti-rational and his impatience with the priests and the church as an institution and attempt to trace Greene's relation to the Christian existentialists. The chapter on Greene's short stories shows that many of the stories contain the same themes as his novels and plays. The third chapter examines the problem of commitment with reference to his later works (*The Quiet American*, *The Comedians*, *The Honorary Consul* and *The Human Factor*). These works are concerned with man's existential freedom and responsibility and bring Greene close to the atheistic existentialists, Sartre and Camus.

The study I have undertaken is all the more fascinating because my task has been to bring out the existential stance of Greene's characters, to harmonize it with his own observations made in autobiographical pieces and to seek its theoretical basis in the existential philosophies of Kierkegaard, Marcel, Buber, Tillich, Sartre and Camus and, whenever possible, to compare and contrast Greene's characters with those of Dostoyevsky, Conrad, Beckett, Sartre and Camus. Thus I have tried to appreciate Greene as a serious writer in search of reality independent of established ethics and values. In striking down all accepted Absolutes, religious and social, which restrict individual freedom, and in insisting on man's need of leading an authentic life, Greene is in the company of existential writers. Like the existentialists, Greene points out that the worn-out values are inadequate, if not completely meaningless, in the face of the widespread sense of life's absurdity and only existentialist values like the worth and dignity of the individual, his freedom of choice and quest for identity have significance. It appears that Greene, consciously or unconsciously, was under the influence of existential ideas popular in the beginning of the present century.

I wish to record my deep sense of gratitude to my revered teacher, mentor and supervisor, Dr. O.P. Mathur, Professor and Head, Department of English, Banaras Hindu University, whose constant help and encouragement saw this work through. He helped me with his scholarly comments and suggestions. I am also grateful to another teacher of mine, Dr. V. Rai, formerly Professor and Head, Department of English, Banaras Hindu University, who helped me whenever help was sought. I also express my thanks to the Librarians and the members of the staff of the Central Library, Banaras Hindu University, the Library of the Department of Philosophy, Banaras Hindu University, Allahabad University Library, Lucknow University Library, Bombay University Library, National Library, Calcutta, and the British Council Library, Calcutta, who helped me in collecting material for my work. My indebtedness to the various biographers and critics of Greene has been recorded in the footnotes in the body of the monograph itself. Finally, I am very grateful to the University Grants Commission for awarding me Teacher Fellowship and to the Government of Orissa, Education and Youth Services Department, for according me permission to avail myself of the fellowship and for treating the period of research as duty.

GANGESHWAR RAI

Notes and References

1. K. Allott and M. Farris, *The Art of Graham Greene* (London: Hamish Hamilton, 1951).
2. Marie Mesnet, *Graham Greene and the Heart of the Matter* (London: The Cresent Press, 1954).
3. John Atkins, *Graham Greene* (London: John Calder, 1957).
4. David Pryce-Jones, *Graham Greene* (London: Oliver and Boyd, 1963).
5. A.A. DeVitis, *Graham Greene* (New York: Twayne Publishers, 1964).
6. F.L. Kunkel, *The Labyrinthine Ways of Greene* (New York, 1960).
7. J. Noxon, "Kierkegaard's Stages and *A Burnt-out Case*", *Review of English Literature*, 3 (1962).
8. Lucio P. Routolo, "*Brighton Rock's* Absurd Heroine", *Modern Language Quarterly*, 25 (1964).
9. R.O. Evans, "Existentialism in Greene's *The Quiet American*", *Modern Fiction Studies*, 3, 3 (1957).
10. Hazel E. Barnes, *The Literature of Possibility: A Study in Humanistic Existentialism* (Lincoln, 1959), p. 380.
11. Graham Greene's personal letter, March 6, 1978.
12. R.O. Evans, ed., *Graham Greene: Some Critical Considerations* (Lexington: University of Kentucky Press, 1967), p. XI.
13. R.W.B. Lewis, "The Fiction of Graham Greene: the Horror and the Glory", *The Kenyon Review*, XIX (Winter 1957), 68.
14. Paul Rosteinne's *Graham Greene: temoinedes temps tragiques* (Paris, 1949), a full-length study in French discusses Greene's novels in terms of Sartrian existentialism.
15. Graham Greene's personal letter to me, March 6, 1978.

Contents

Preface v

Contents ix

Introduction: The Shaping of the Vision 1

1. The Beginning of the Quest 19

2. The Existential Christian 30

3. The Existential Humanist 72

4. Hints of a Vision: Short Stories 105

5. Hints of a Vision: Plays 122

Conclusion 139

Select Bibliography 145

Index 159

Introduction

The Shaping of the Vision

GRAHAM GREENE observed in an interview, "A novelist cannot write about anything of which he has not had direct personal experience."[1] Greene's life and work have a synergetic relationship reinforcing and fulfilling each other. The autobiographical revelations in his miscellaneous writings evince an existential bias which has welled up from his own personal vision.

Graham Greene, the fourth of the six children of the same parents, was brought up in a comfortable bourgeois intellectual background. The family represented all that was most able in the English professional class. There was no loneliness to be experienced in his parents' old, spacious house crowded with people—"six children, a Nanny, a nurse-maid, a gardener, a fat and cheerful cook, a beloved head-housemaid, a platoon of assistant maids".[2] These hordes were not swallowed up by the spaciousness of it all: a vast garden with shaded walks and herbaceous borders, a croquet lawn and a revolving summer house, kitchen gardens and green houses. This was a dream world, in short, of ease, calm and decorum. Only in the clouds ahead he could see that "There was no luminosity at all."[3] His father, who was the headmaster of Berkhemsted School, was always shut up in his study working on the time-table or reading and so inaccessible to his children. Greene felt very little affection for him and as a young man deliberately set out to hurt the sentiment of his father whose idea was "unflinchingly liberal in politics and gently conservative in morals".[4] Greene was separated from his mother by the presence of servants. His mother was rational, kind, cold and practical. Far from being a Fabian, but with a similar chilled good sense "she seemed to eliminate all confusion, to recognize the good from the bad and choose the good, though where her family was concerned in later years she noticed only the good".[5] Distrustful of the supernatural that is so natural to children, she may well have been a model for the mother in his play *The Potting Shed.* The real centre of the boy's emotional life was Nanny, an old woman, who was pensioned off and became more remote than even his father and mother. Her devotion and service earn a brief paragraph in Greene's autobiography: "I remember her bent over my bath with her white hair in a bun, holding a sponge. Her temper deteriorated before she retired on a pension, but I never remember being afraid of her, only impressed by that white bun of age."[6] Thus the sense of abandonment by parents which is a part of the lost childhood of so many of his fictional characters has stemmed from his own experience. The feeling of loneliness is a very remarkable theme which Greene has presented in *The Man Within*, *England Made Me*, *Brighton Rock*, and in plays like *The Potting Shed* and *Carving a Statue*, and in stories like "The Basement Room" and "Under the Garden."

At the age of thirteen Greene was packed off to the expensive squalid world of the boarding school. Although he was, in fact, a pupil in his father's establishment, the family home was just across the road, he found himself in a strange world. The home was at once home and school separated by a "baize door" from the outside world. Greene lived restlessly on the border. The instant coming and going between two different environments was a strain on the sensitive boy and encouraged a nostalgia for lawless roads. The chapter on his school days in the autobiography begins with his trying unsuccessfully to cut his "right leg open with a penknife".[7] This was an outcome of his terrible boredom he experienced in a "savage country of strange customs and inexplicable cruelties".[8] Here he was a foreigner and a suspect, a hunted creature having dubious associates. Being the headmaster's son, he was detached from other boys who took him to be a "Quisling". He was surrounded by the forces of the resistance, and yet he could not join them without betraying his father and brother. Certain items in the school routine awfully disgusted him. He was "very bad at gymnastics"[9] and all his life his instinct has been to abandon anything for which he has no talent. In order to avoid the class held in the gym, he pretended to be ill. He would secretly walk up to the common with a book of his interest and stay there hidden. Truancy became a pattern of his life: "The danger of discovery lent those hours a quality of excitement which was very close to momentary happiness."[10] School rules—the haphazard methods of "the censorship of books from home, . . . the lavatories without locks . . . Sunday walks"[11] in unwanted company roused nausea in Greene. As no one was allowed to walk alone on Sunday afternoons, Greene had to beg with a bitter sense of humiliation for the inclusion of his name in groups who had no desire for his company. Of course, after a term or two of purgatory, he received permission of his parents to spend Sunday afternoons at home. O.T.C. parade was another item in the routine which Greene hated most. He felt uneasy in the prescribed uniform and dreaded the parades where he always "fumbled fixing bayonets or strayed forming fours".[12] He endured this life of monotony, humiliation and mental pain for some eight terms —a hundred and four weeks. He was helped by his truancies, those peaceful hours hidden in the hedge. But unhappiness was a daily routine. He felt like a man condemned to a long prison sentence. The deprivation of boarding school life, comfortless and utterly without privacy—"loneliness, the struggle of conflicting loyalties, the sense of continuous grime",[13] roused the first act of rebellion. The quisling took to the maquis, ran away from school and hid out on the common, only to be humiliatingly ambushed after a few hours by his elder sister. His father, a decent understanding man, took his son's misery seriously. On the advice of an elder brother, who was a medical student, Graham was sent to a London psychoanalyst with whom he spent "perhaps the happiest six months"[14] of his life. In 1920, it was an astonishing decision to make for a mildly conservative parent. The psychoanalysis, however, was not much fruitful. The most effective aspect of the treatment was the simple change of scene; Greene was sixteen free and in London. But he continued to lapse into boredom even after this psychoanalysis. He could take no aesthetic interest in any visual thing. He felt nothing staring at a beautiful sight because he was fixed in boredom "like a negative in a chemical bath".[15] Greene's despairing passion for his sister's governess, who was engaged to be married to another man, temporarily eased the burden of boredom: he lived only "for the moments with her".[16] The agonizing crisis of boredom reached an intolerable depth and he had to try out other methods of escape. A few years earlier he had attempted suicide on four occasions, by drinking "a quantity of hypo under the false impression that it was poisonous", by draining his "blue glass bottle of hay-fever drops", by eating "a bunch of deadly night-shade" and by swallowing "twenty aspirins before swimming in the empty school baths".[17] None of these were attempts at suicide, they were only gambles with death. Later, at Oxford, alcohol began to appeal to him "in the innocent form of bitter beer".[18] He used it for one entire term as an alleviation of boredom-sickness. He was drunk from breakfast to bed. Terror was another weapon to conquer boredom. First, he took to frightening himself on horseback. He writes: "I would take a horse out only in order to scare myself with jumps on the common and escape the deep boredom."[19] Then he played Russian Roulette with his brother's revolver to rescue himself from the abyss of despair. Atkins aptly remarks: "Greene used his revolver as Huxley used mescalin to induce dimensions of spiritual experience which would be otherwise acquired only through the accidents of one's personal life."[20] He went to the common with his brother's revolver and pulled the trigger of the revolver with one of its six chambers loaded, not knowing whether he would shoot himself with the loaded chamber. The game had the effect of an exhilarating drug. He had "an extra-ordinary sense of jubilation. . . heart knocked in its cage, and life contained an infinite number of possibilities. It was like a young man's first experience of sex."[21] Greene discovered the possibility of enjoying again the visible world by risking its total loss. The imminence of death could revive the will to live. Greene writes: "When the human mind has for some time been fluctuating between hope and despair, tortured with anxiety, and humid from one extreme to another, it affords a sort of gloomy relief to know the worst that can possibly happen . . . ."[22] This reminds us of Sartre who believes that the risk of death affects and enriches the spirit. Sartre remarks: "I was looking at my life through my death . . . I learned to bear grief and sickness; in them I saw the beginning of my triumphal death . . . I accepted the worst as the condition of the best."[23] Colin Wilson refers to this margin of human consciousness that can be stimulated by pain, but not by pleasure, as the "indifference threshold". For convenience he also refers to it as "The St. Neot margin".[24]

For several years Greene periodically repeated the game until he found he was not even excited. He gave up playing Russian Roulette, but a kind of Russian Roulette, an instinct to get beyond boredom contriving the sense of terror, remained a factor even in his later life. He was busy with other plans, but the war against boredom went on. He went to Liberia, to Tobasco during the religious persecution, to a leproserie in the Cango, to Kikuyu, to Malaya and to Vietnam. There in those last three regions of clandestine wars, the fear of ambush served him "as effectively as the Russian Roulette in the life-long war against boredom".[25] It is not with Greene alone, the urge to escape from selfhood and the environment is present in most of the persons and for most of the time. Aldous Huxley observes: "Most men and women lead lives at the worst so painful, at the best so monotonous, poor and limited that the urge to escape, the longing to transcend themselves if only for a few moments, is and has always been one of the principal appetites of the soul."[26]

The Liberian journey, an important event in his life, settled things once and for all and gave him the full and final shape of his vision. Greene went to Liberia, as Henry James did to Europe, in a moment of creative crisis in order to experience a richer reality. The devil-dance, other terrors and fierce cruelties, both natural and human, led to an acute sensation of pleasure and both as a man and as a writer, he came back alive from Liberia. The danger of the journey revealed in him something he had not been aware of possessing, a love of life. He was deeply stirred by the bareness of the African's needs. The experience of terror and pleasure and their supernatural source inspired in him quite unexpectedly an interest in living. It was significantly like a "conversion". The revelation of value, indeed the very possibility of living against the absorption of death, came with the shock of conversion: "I had discovered in myself a passionate interest in living. I had always assumed before, as a matter of course, that death was desirable."[27]

After formal education, Greene was no longer willing to depend on his parents who had given him everything they could. He was anxious to find employment and bear personal responsibility for his whole future about which he describes his worries: "Now it was my turn to decide and no one—not even the Oxford Appointments Board—could help me very far. I was hemmed in by a choice of jails in which to serve my life imprisonment."[28]

After trying a few short-lived jobs—he worked in the British-American Tobacco Company for two weeks and then took up a private tutoring job for some time—he settled down to journalism. His boredom still haunted him. Once he was so bored that he had a perfectly good tooth pulled out only for a whiff of ether: "A few minutes unconsciousness was like a holiday from the world. I had lost a good tooth, but the boredom was for the time being dispersed."[29] For three years he worked on the *Nottingham Journal* and eventually on *The Times*. During these years he was engaged to be married to Vivien, a Roman Catholic girl, and this induced his conversion to Catholicism. In order to marry the Catholic girl, he felt that he should "learn the nature and limits of the beliefs she held".[30] He received instructions from Father Trollope and, having been convinced of the probability of the existence of God, accepted Catholicism. His conversion was by reason alone: "...there was no joy in it at all, only a sombre apprehension. I had made the first move with a view to future marriage."[31] A little before marriage Greene suffered from appendicitis and had to undergo operation. After two weeks he reported for duty. As he returned too soon, he fainted on his first evening at work and was wrongly diagnosed as epileptic. The term roused great terror. As the disease is hereditary requiring a careful consideration of the matter before marriage, he was upset by the thought of starting an altogether different future than the one he had planned. He thought of suicide but had not the courage to do it. Then he went to Father Talbot with the hope that he would relieve him of his anxiety. Though the priest was a man of great human sympathy, he had no solution for Greene. Greene leaped into the future and married. The event bred distrust in the priests and probably this is the reason why he has made his clerical characters, Father Rank in *The Heart of the Matter* and Father James in *The Living Room*, fail before the human problems.

As soon as Greene was established on *The Times*, his first successful novel, *The Man Within*, was accepted for publication. Greene had a choice to make between journalism and novel-writing. He chose the latter against the advice of his well-wishers but regretted his decision in the years to come when he fell on evil days. He was back to failure, to the gloomy country of his heart. His next two novels were reluctantly accepted. The money he had earned from his first novel was exhausted after three years. He could not even land on a journalistic job. Both *The Spectator* and *The Catholic Herald* turned him down. He applied for a job in Chulankaran University (near Bangkok). *Stamboul Train*, published as *Orient Express* in America, saved him. Isolation, feeling of boredom and failure are the recurring themes of Greene's novels because they have been the recurrent themes of his life too. He thoroughly depends on the experiences of his life for the material of his novels. Greene believes: "A writer's knowledge of himself, realistic and unromantic, is like a store of energy on which he must draw for a life-time: one volt of it properly directed will bring a character alive."[32]

This brief survey of the important events of Greene's life reveals a close relationship between his life and work. His works are laden by the bitter memories of his school life—the horrible confinement and the prison-like condition—"the memories of flight, rebellion and misery during those first sixteen years when the novelist is formed".[33] Greene, like Marcel to whom "Nothing is more dangerous for spiritual development than boredom",[34] thinks that "tiredness and anxiety and homesickness can turn the heart to stone as easily as cruelty, sin, the violent act, the rejection of God".[35] Greene, like Camus, Moravia and Malraux, insists on the significance of man's struggle to escape boredom and experience the fullness of life when the opposite inclination, the radical bias towards death, is almost equally vehement.

Greene is full of indignation against the present social institutions which aim at creating mass-men and attach no importance to man as the individual. As it is by efforts of his own that Greene could settle his account with the past and come to terms with whatever wounds there were, he insists on the significance of the freedom and conscious independent initiative of the individual. His Liberian trip, that he recounts in *Journey Without Maps*, was a protest against the present-day civilization that was largely responsible for the maladies that afflicted him all through his life. It is Greene's own knowledge of life that has led him to criticize, like Kierkegaard and Jaspers, the devitalizing effects of life in the present century. His journey in Liberia "represented a distrust of any future based on what we are . . .".[36] He mourns the loss of a world, of a condition wherein "the sense of taste was finer, the sense of pleasure keener, the sense of terror deeper and purer,"[37] a place now lost in the glitter of the chromium plate of the modern civilized society, except for a few primitive portions of the earth. Stressing that the present welfare systems cannot give spiritual peace to man, Greene, like Conrad, pleads for a return to the "bareness simplicity, instinctive friendliness, feeling rather than thought, and start again . . . ."[38]

Like Kierkegaard's Abraham, Greene himself suffered from doubts and uncertainty and found it very hard "to believe in a God at all".[39] Neither his conversion to Roman Catholicism nor philosophical arguments could help him to reach living faith. The image of Father Talbot, who failed to help Greene in the terrible moments of his life, recurs in his works which reveal his usual impatience with Catholic dogma and the Church's teachings. *Brighton Rock*, *The Power and the Glory*, *The Heart of the Matter*, *The End of the Affair* and his plays, *The Living Room* and *The Potting Shed*, reflect his distrust in organized religion—the church and its rituals—as they deprive man of his freedom and existential humanity. Greene denounces conventional piety and the formal aspects of religion because they tend to drive out the essentials—love for God and love for a corrupt and suffering humanity. Faith, to Greene, is unconditioned and unconditional. It is the free movement of the heart and it comes to one "shapelessly, without dogma...".[40] Greene's heroes acquire faith without observing the rules of the church. Greene's view of faith comes close to Kierkegaard's, who was angry at Christianity being reduced to a conventionalized institution, which he regards as an apostacy, for it takes away all true decisions and deep seriousness of the leap to faith. To Kierkegaard faith is a miracle, it is the highest passion of mankind. It flows out of man's "inwardness"[41] and it is without objective evidence. Greene, like Kierkegaard, emphasizes the paradoxical nature of faith.

Greene's writings confirm his inclination towards the mysterious and the irrational in life. His own life is a witness to the uniqueness of the individual and the presence of the illogical in life. No one of his brothers, though with similar upbringing and education as Graham Greene's, lived a schizophrenic life like him. Raymond distinguished himself as a physician and a mountaineer, Hugh became the Director-General of the B.B.C. and Carleton, a famous columnist, organized the campaign to bring back the Nine O'Clock news through the columns of *The Times*. If Greene were "a maniac-depressive"[42] like his grandfather, psychoanalysis did not cure his condition. This speaks of the illogicality of life. As they failed in his own case, Greene appears to be disappointed at the scientific and technological achievements of modern man and his attempt to fit everything into logic. He believes in the force of the irrational and criticizes the progressive liberal outlook that seeks to improve life through mental guidance and social engineering. He believes that life will be "happier with the enormous supernatural promise than with the petty social fulfilment, the tiny pension and the machine-made furniture".[43] Greene emphasizes the significance of man's inner being that stands beyond the grasp of human intellect and repudiates the present emphasis on rationalism as limited and inadequate for a full understanding of man.

Thus Greene has been an existential man, haunted and anguished in his life. He has been absolutely alone and free choosing his way of life out of chaos and uncertain future. He is thus one of the contemporary writers about whom Nathan A. Scott observes: "Indeed all the great literature of the modern period might be said to be a literature of metaphysical isolation for the modern artist—and this is perhaps the fundamental truth about him—has experienced a great loneliness, the kind of loneliness that is known by the soul when it has to undertake, unaided by ministries either of church or of culture, the adventure of discovering fundamental principles of meaning."[44] Like the existentialists, Greene points out that the extra singularity of each individual makes his problem and way unique and that any deviation forced with a view to conforming to a pre-established pattern proves disastrous. He pleads for the individual's existential freedom that entails care and concern for others.

Notes and References

1. *The Hindustan Times*: *Sunday Magazine*, September 29, 1957, p. 1, col. 3.
2. Graham Greene, *A Sort of Life* (London: Bodley Head, 1971), Penguin Books, 1972, p. 52.
3. *Ibid.*, p. 53. 4. *Ibid.*, p. 20. 5. *Ibid.*, p. 15.
6. *Ibid.*, p. 22. 7. *Ibid.*, p. 54. 8. *Ibid.*
9. *Ibid.*, p. 48. 10. *Ibid.*, pp. 55-6. 11. *Ibid.*, p. 58.
12. *Ibid.*, p. 62. 13. *Ibid.*, p. 59. 14. *Ibid.*, p. 72.
15. *Ibid.*, p. 93. 16. *Ibid.*, p. 90. 17. *Ibid.*, p. 64.
18. *Ibid.*, p. 87. 19. *Ibid.*, p. 78.
20. John Atkins, *Graham Greene*, p. 190.
21. *A Sort of Life*, p. 94.
22. Graham Greene, "Books in General", *New Statesman*, June 2, 1952, p. 745.
23. Jean-Paul Sartre, *Words*, trans. Irene Clephane (London: Hamish Hamilton, 1964), Penguin Books, 1967, p. 145.
24. Colin Wilson, *Beyond The Outsider* (London: Pan Books Ltd., 1965), p. 32.
25. *A Sort of Life*, p. 96.
26. Aldoux Huxley, *The Doors of Perception* (London: Chatto & Windus, 1954), Penguin Books, 1965, p. 51.
27. Graham Greene, *Journey Without Maps* (London: William Heinemann Ltd., 1936), Penguin Books, 1976, p. 213.
28. *A Sort of Life*, p. 106.
29. *Ibid.*, p. 113. 30. *Ibid.*, p. 118. 31. *Ibid.*, 122.
32. *Ibid.*, p. 147. 33. *Ibid.*
34. Gabriel Marcel, *Metaphysical Journal*, trans. Bernard Wall (Chicago: Henry Regnery Company, 1952), p. 236.
35. Graham Greene, *The Lawless Roads* (London: William Heinemann Ltd., 1939), Penguin Books, 1976, p. 157.
36. *Journey Without Maps*, p. 20.
37. *Ibid.*, pp. 224-25. 38. *Ibid.*, p. 192.
39. "I didn't disbelieve in Christ—I disbelieved in God. If I were to be convinced in even the remote possibility of a supreme,

omnipotent and omniscient power I realized that nothing afterwards could seem impossible. It was on the ground of a dogmatic atheism that I fought and fought hard. It was like a fight for personal survival." *A Sort of Life*, p. 120.

40. *The Lawless Roads*, p. 14.
41. "The paradox of faith is that there is an inwardness in terms of the external. . . ." Kierkegaard, *Fear and Trembling,* trans. Robert Payne and W. Lowrie (New York: Doubleday, 1954), p. 89.
42. *A Sort of Life*, p. 92.
43. *The Lawless Roads*, p. 49.
44. "The Broken Centre: A Definition of the Crisis of Values in Modern Literature", *Chicago Review*, No. 2, XIII (Summer 1959), 188.

CHAPTER ONE

The Beginning of the Quest

THE early novels of Graham Greene reflect aspects of the existential diagnosis of contemporary life. What one confronts in life today, is a tragic alienation and dehumanization of man who is living in a poisoned cultural milieu. In spite of all he has achieved by way of civilization, he always suffers from a sense of rootlessness, lack of purpose and insignificance. The individual feels isolated because the flow of information between his environment and himself has been absolutely stopped. The adaptive function of the individual has been put out of joint in relation to himself as well as others. He can neither reach and understand himself nor grasp his world. Graham Greene is critical of the alienating factors that prevail in modern society and stresses the pointlessness of human existence. He also insists on alienation as a form of spiritual dyspepsia. There is no alienating situation in itself. A man may live out his condition as one that alienates whereas another exactly in the same position may not have this experience. The feeling of alienation rises from within and a man can rid himself of it for he is free.

The Man Within (1929) is Greene's first published novel which explores the theme of man's double nature. Leslie Paul observes: "Man is divided in himself... Division and disharmony are the signs ef man's spiritual stature. For he is not only divided, he is aware of being divided against himself."[1] The issues of the divided mind, sin and repentance, are very explicitly presented through the contending higher and lower natures of the protagonist. Andrews is a typical Greene hero or anti-hero who is an isolated man with a sense of overwhelming desolation and who finds "himself friendless and alone".[2] The lonely man has to live with the angry man inside. He declares: "...he is made up of two persons, the sentimental, bullying, desiring child and another more stern critic."[3] He is conscious of his failure "to exist", his lack of personality. He cannot get beyond the surface of himself, his sincerity goes no further than a simple awareness of all the tendencies warring in his mind. The opposed forces of his natural desires, and the exigency of his inner self "the man within" at constant war with each other for supremacy, have set his mind in turmoil. His alienation from the world of peace and happiness makes his plight even worse. His eyes are filled with tears at a vision of "little grey churches, corn fields, stiles, honeyed distant bells in the dusk, robins in snow".[4] The feeling of loneliness and the sense of having lost his haven, even the haven of his own self, frighten him: "There was nothing in him but sentiment and fear and cowardice, nothing in him but negatives. How could anyone believe in him if he did not even exist."[5]

The novel is full of flashbacks which reveal Andrews's hidden past. The memory of his unhappy childhood and overbearing father always haunts him. He remembers his father, who was "domineering, brutal, a conscious master, not chary of his blows to either child or wife".[6] He calls his father "a bully", who "killed his wife and ruined his son"[7] and who put Andrews at a school to learn irrelevant subjects like Greek, just to brag about it. Andrews blames his father and lack of integrated education for what he is: "It's not a man's fault. . . It's all in the way he's born. . . I didn't make myself."[8] Greene is careful to suggest that Andrews's situation does not entirely determine the course of his career. Though influenced by the environment, he is free to choose his course of action. When extremely sick of school life, barren of any object of affection, he runs away from it as Graham Greene himself had done. It is Andrews who "insisted that Carlyon must come down to the school and make arrangements".[9] After his father's death, he hopes for peace and freedom from fear and joins the gang of the smugglers but there is no change. The ghost of his father follows him on board. His father is a model against which he is measured and found wanting. He has the sense of being left out, slightly victimized, not quite treated as one of the gang. He finds himself "on suffrance. . . treated with contempt"[10] whose opinion is never consulted. He seeks to assert himself as someone who is to be considered and who has the power to smash all their plans. Driven by jealousy and hatred, he betrays his friends to the excisemen. Moreover, he is aware of the void within and is anxious to fill it. When Elizabeth asks him, "Is there anything you care for or went?" he replies, "to be null and void".[11] The state aspired to, is described as listening to music. He says: "For years I have longed for a peace, a certainty, a sanity. I thought I could get it perhaps in music."[12]

Andrews's problem like those of Greene himself and of his later heroes is to come to terms with himself. He resolves to act in sincerity with himself and forgets all about it the next moment. On his way to the court to give witness against his friends, he falls to Lucy, a woman of loose morals. But he has a feeling of horror in the wake of corruption and feels the whole weight of his betrayal of the new life in which he would learn courage and even self-forgetfulness. He says: "I've wallowed... I was a fool and imagined I was escaping, but now I have sunk so deep that I've reached the bottom."[13] Unable to understand his disgust and despair, Lucy guesses wrongly that he will not return to Elizabeth: "I thought you were going to rescue that girl of yours from danger. Why don't you go? It's ridiculous to sit on the edge of a bed naked and philosophize."[14] He returns to Elizabeth in spite of danger to himself. The desire to raise himself from the dirt is stronger and the fear of pain and death is cast out by a greater fear—"a terror of life, of going on soiling himself and repeating and soiling himself again".[15] In her presence, he is relieved of his gnawing sense of fear, he acts courageously, and decides to stay with her. He loses even the fear of death and reaches the moment of awakening after her death. Before her death his self-realization has been only momentary. Her death nerves him to a willing acceptance of his own. His divided self is made whole and he feels happy and at peace, for his father in him is slain and his true self is now freed from lust, blasphemy and cowardice. He identifies himself with the "man within": "His father's had been a stubborn ghost, but it was laid at last, and he need no longer be torn in two between that spirit and the stern unresting critic which was wont to speak. I am that critic, he said with a sense of discovery and exhilaration."[16] Through the character of Andrews, Greene seems to stress that an experience of terror helps to come morally alive. The immersion in the destructive element saves him by destroying him. He proves the truth of Colin Wilson's view expressed in the following statement: "...so long a man is not horrified at himself, he knows nothing about himself."[17]

If the sense of terror is what may bring a man to life, it is love of a rather special order that can fulfil him. Elizabeth is one of the few wholly good characters Greene has drawn. To Andrews, "she is a saint"[18] "as holy as a vision",[19] and she gives "a meaning and a possibility to holiness and divinity".[20] Her beauty and holiness evoke in him a love that for once is not lust. In her presence, he feels a sense of trust and friendliness to which he has been a stranger. Her goodness lifts him out of the mire of sin, and strengthens his spirit against flesh. He is really alive at the close of the novel when he is taken away to be executed for a murder he has not committed but confesses to have done so as to save the life of his comrade. He feels happy and at peace because he is at one with his deeper self and realizes the inner vision. The love of Elizabeth which combines with the stimulus of terror leads him to this state of self-realization and gives him a glimpse of the ultimate source of existence.

Man's potentialities are hidden in his true self, and his body and private acts which we perceive are not the real person. The real person is revealed in his dreams which are "potentialities, aspects, and no man could tell whether suddenly and without warning they might not take control and turn the coward for one instant into the hero".[21] A man authenticates his existence by discovering his active inner self. He realizes his potentialities beyond the passing impulse of the moment by choosing to be what the really is. In the process of self-discovery, man creates himself. A man must attend to the inner call and answer it courageously in order to achieve authentic existence. Limited and individualized, a man is conditioned by his environment, by his past, his nature too. He, however, is free to accept his situation in his own way. His freedom lies in his power to transcend the situation in which he has been placed. He freely chooses and so orients his life in the line of his destiny. His situation is only the concrete material given to him as a test. Elizabeth lives authentically. Instead of surrendering herself to determinism, she lives in agreement with her conscience. Andrews, on the other hand, seems to be a victim of what Colin Wilson calls "indifference threshold" or "St. Neot Margin"[22] Andrews's vitality is asleep. When a sense of terror combined with love goes deep enough to shake his mind, he achieves real life with the mind awake.

In *The Man Within*, Greene presents the drama of Andrews's conscience and one has the impression that the visible world has been neglected. *It's a Battlefield* is concerned with many cruel and ugly aspects of life in the thirties. Men and women as they are conditioned by our industrialized life are treated and the novel seems to have a sociological concern. But Greene is actually more interested in individual destinies than in the improvement of society. His social and political interest always comes next to his interest in the problems of man as the individual. An individual's sense of loneliness, anxiety and the meaninglessness of human life are the important issues which are very powerfully projected in this novel.

The epigraph of the novel, a passage from Kingslake's *Eothen*, describes a battlefield made up of "small numberless circlets... each separate gathering of English soldiery went on fighting its own little battle in happy and advantageous ignorance of the general state of the action; nay, even very often in ignorance of the fact that any great conflict was raging".[23] Greene sees the world as a battlefield in which a number of people are involved. The action moves round Jim Drover, a bus-driver sentenced to death for killing a policeman at a riotous Communist meeting. The plot is immediately concerned to show the reactions of a miscellany of beings to this particular situation. They fight in utter ignorance of what is happening around them. No one wants Jim to die but no one, except for the Assistant Commissioner, is sure of what he wants. They are apparently worried about Drover, but really they are interested in themselves and their actions are determined by their selfishness. Conrad and Milly strive to help him and are driven to betray him, Kay Rimmer and Jules Briton forget all about Drover for their unsatisfactory love makings. Surrogate does not himself practise what he preaches. This is a world inhabited by men of limited vision. Lynne Chenney remarks: "Although there are innumerable struggles occurring in this world, each man is aware only of his own, and any larger battle of which his own struggle might be a part, remains mystery to him."[24]

The action is set in a shabby background. The setting affects very much the lives of the characters. Here we have certain important features of modern city life—dirty flats with hair combings, rooms with a "smell of stale air and dead bats on the floor,"[25] brothels which spring up "like mushrooms overnight in the most unlikely places",[26] factories, where "Between death and disfigurement, unemployment and the streets, between the cog-wheels and the shafting," the girls stand as the hands of the clock move "round from eight in the morning until one (milk and biscuits at eleven) and then the long drag to six,"[27] prisons with A, B and C blocks, which remind one of the circles of hell, evening papers, giving news of rape and murder, political meetings, riots and suppression, young tinted faces of women, overworked and without any future, giggling and chattering through "dust dark and degradation". This is a chaotic and irrational world of material poverty and spiritual emptiness where nothing happens up to man's expectations. People, engaged in a battle, represent different aspects of dereliction. The goodness of Mrs. Coney and the faith of Caroline Bury are ineffective. It stretches on all sides of characters, isolating them: "Loneliness was only too easily attained; it was in the air one breathed; open any door, it opened on to loneliness in the passage, close the door at night, one shut loneliness in. The toothbrush, the chair, the ewer and the bed were dents in loneliness. One had only to stop, to stare, to listen, and one was lost. Then sorrow gripped him for all the useless suffering he could do nothing to ease."[28] The action and the setting remind one of Conrad's *The Secret Agent*. Comparing the two novels, Atkins aptly remarks: "The same sordidness, the same bitterness and dark intensity run through both of them, there is the same sense of defeat, of hopelessness, despite the occasional experiences of implications of hope."[29]

Mr. Surrogate is a Communist who lives all alone in his comfortable flat. The portrait of his dead artist-wife hanging in his room "as an atonement for his dislike, as a satisfaction for humility",[30] reminds him of his wife who had never failed to see through him and whose domestic disappointment led her to painting: "She was angry with him and this was her way of baiting him. Of course her dissatisfaction made her as an artist."[31] Though he declares his respect for his dead wife and refrains from bedding with the attractive and willing Kay Rimmer for a while, he seduces the girl and feels shame afterwards. Mr. Surrogate, who in his own eyes is a public figure, the most advanced thinker in the country, feels that a girl like Kay is not really fit for him, and resolves to be faithful to his dead wife: "I have done you enough harm, Margaret. I'll be faithful. I'll give this girl up."[32] Communism provides an escape from his lust, shame, betrayal and cowardice. He enthusiastically talks of abstractions—social betterment, equality of opportunity, means of production. But he has no love for man as the individual. He avoids actual contacts with human beings and needs a companion just to talk and confirm his views on capitalism and socialism, wealth and poverty. But he is careful lest someone may look into his human weakness and spoil his public image: "... the lovely abstractions of Communism had lured him into the party—Comradeship, Proletariat, Ideology .... He resented even Drover's intrusion as an individual to be saved and not a sacrifice to be decked for the altar . . . individuals gave pain by their brutality, their malice, their lack of understanding. He could live in a world of religions, of political parties and economic creeds, he would go mad rubbing shoulders at every turn with saviours, politicians, poor people begging bread."[33] A fake Communist, he preaches sacrifice but illustrates his inability to practise it. Greene's Communists do not believe either in themselves or in their theories, they are like rats behind wainscoting. Greene appears to be stressing the need of a genuine revolutionary leader who actually lives the ideals and points out that Mr. Surrogate is only a poor substitute.

Conder, a journalist living in a squalid bed-sitting-room, is really a seedy lonely man dissatisfied with his pay, profession and life. Sad and depressed, he conjures up impersonations of a revolutionary, the intimate of Scotland Yard and a family man. On account of his habit of make-believe he loses contact with reality. He is aware of the irrationality of the world: "The world, he thought. . . was run by the whims of a few men, the whims of a politician, a journalist, a bishop and a policeman. They hanged this man and pardoned that; one embezzler was in prison but other men of the same kind were sent to Parliament. . . but he knew well enough that it was not systematic enough to be called injustice."[34]

Kay Rimmer is a pretty promiscuous factory girl, who is employed in Battersea match factory where one hundred and fifty girls work "with the regularity of the blood beat"[35] from dawn to dusk. In order to escape from the dull and drab routine of life, she has tried everything—art, politics, church. She attends Communist gatherings not out of political interest but because she knows that at these gatherings "there would be fifty men to every woman."[36] She feels that she must do something to help her sister Milly, but she is afraid of losing her job. Moreover, sex being irresistible to her, she comes alive in the moment of copulation: "Her body was ready for enjoyment; the deep peace of sensuality covered all the fears and perplexities of the day; she never felt more at home than in a bed or a man's arms."[37] Her lover, Jules Briton, another dehumanized figure in the novel, feels bored and is in search of a cause to live. He is painfully aware of his joyless and rootless existence and admires people who do not wrangle for leadership but readily and patiently follow others. The legacy of ten thousand francs from his father does not bring about any change in his life. He has second thoughts about sharing his life and fortune with Kay and about working to obtain signatures on the petition for Drover's release. He makes himself miserable when left alone. He is prepared to pay anything he has for company: "... he was desperate for a place in the world, a task, a duty. But give him voices, company, and he was happy, he was cocksure, he was vulgar, he showed off."[38] He is, thus, Heidegger's "das man" anxious to lose himself in the crowd.

Milly and Conrad are the only characters who are directly involved in the "battlefield" and who sincerely wish to help Drover. Milly, living all alone in her basement, and her husband whom she loves and with whom communication is barred, in jail, are "like two countries at war, with the telegraph wires down, and the rails torn up".[39] The thought of empty years ahead as a result of a life sentence for her husband stupefies her: "She felt it like the withering of the skin, the death of her sex. When he came out of prison she would be without passion or enjoyment."[40] She feels defenceless, against the importunities of the world. The idea of happiness in the absurd and hostile world frightens her: "No one likes people to be happy. If we hadn't been so happy, he wouldn't be there... we'd be together. I never wanted to be happy. I was always afraid."[41] She desperately seeks for some way of saving her husband and faces an existence similar to that of a rebel.

Conrad Drover, the chief Insurance Clerk and the winner of scholarship, is Greene's first serious treatment of a recurrent type. Being regularly promoted to the higher ranks on the basis of his intelligence and efficiency, he is now indispensable to the office. But he is trained to only "adding and subtracting, multiplying and dividing".[42] His intelligence that brought him through examinations and earned him a well-paid job does not help him in a crisis. Milly's dependence upon him renders him "dizzy with fear".[43] His preoccupation with figures has atrophied his natural capacities for spontaneous response which could carry him through critical situations. Conrad who is overworked and conditioned by big business suffers from isolation caused by his intelligence: "Brains, like a fierce heat, had turned the world to a desert round him, and across the sands in the occasional mirage he saw the stupid crowds, playing, laughing, and without thought enjoying the tenderness, the compassion, the companionship of love."[44] He has a sense of insignificance in the world which appears to him hideous and idiotic and where everything goes by influence. He sincerely wishes to help

Milly and the sense of powerlessness fills him with hatred and guilt. At times he even hates his brother for the plight fallen on him: "I am fond of him. But he's making me hate him. I've got to hate somebody for this."[45] He hates those who deny him happiness. The feelings of powerlessness, loneliness and a sense of pity drive him to bed with Milly: "It was the unexcitement in his love, the element of pity, that kept him there. It seemed unbearable to him that she should suffer."[46] But after the act he has a sense of injury they have done to each other and feels the pinch of his conscience. He has to undergo an ordeal of self-condemnation and despair. The feeling of guilt and hatred rouses in his mind a state of morbidity. His hatred is concentrated on the Assistant Commissioner who signifies a civilization, law, justice and a way of life which Conrad sees as a cause of his agony. Conrad thinks that a word from him would save his brother and desperately seeks to rid himself of his obsessions killing him. This is also an attempt to assert his manhood and redeem his failure. But ironically he is knocked down by a car and dies in the hospital in full awareness of his helplessness and failure. His effort to shoot the Assistant Commissioner ends in his own death. Conrad is a "rebel"[47] in the sense Camus has used the term. An obedient insurance clerk, he revolts when he confronts with the absurdity of existence and his death confirms the absurdity of life.

Caroline Bury and the Assistant Commissioner, who fight the battle in their own ways, are "best equipped to see into the real issues".[48] Having a passion for art, poetry and painting and having no illusion about life, Caroline Bury sees life in all its absurdity, waste and suffering. She is aware of the aimlessness of existence as keenly as the Assistant Commissioner but she chooses a different way out. Pain being unbearable to her, she is worried and unwilling to see people. Frightened of human suffering, she is unable to "stand pain".[49] It is embarrassing to die now "with the world in the state it is", if one hasn't "faith".[50] She has an unshakable faith but in what it is impossible to know. She bemuses herself with incense, idols, ikons. The Assistant Commissioner who is envious of her faith observes: ". . . it's lucky she has got faith, whatever she means by it, she's got nothing else."[51] Caroline Bury represents the existential attitude which is "philosophical suicide"[52] in Camus, an evasion of the absurdity of life.

The Assistant Commissioner is the most disinterested and

inarticulate character in the novel. His nature, training and profession in the East isolate him from the London flux. He finds himself in an alien world and fails to "understand this place".[53] He lives alone in his apartment "surrounded by the comforting accumulated rubbish of his life, the native weapons, the pipe racks, the decorated gourds. . .".[54] He is separated from his subordinates who resent his presence and interference in the affairs of their department. His only refuge from his loneliness of life is his job. He clings to it as "the only thing it was certainly right to do".[55] In his devotion to duty he anticipates the unamed Lieutenant in *The Power and the Glory*. But the Lieutenant believes in the validity of the system he is upholding whereas the Assistant Commissioner has no such belief. The widespread injustice, brutality and perversion embarrass him and block the working of his mind. In a mood of depression he longs to serve an organization which were just, fair and reasonable. But the highest motive he can offer is that of doing his job. He knows that in a life full of contradictions and moral maxims which do not apply, "it is impossible for a man to found his life on any higher motive than doing his job".[56] He reminds us of Conrad's Jim "whose only reward is in the perfect love of the work".[57] He feels old and dusty, and the thought of retirement and old age chills his heart. It will mean the loss of his only value, the only justification of his dehydrated existence. The administration of justice conflicts with his natural sympathy: "His enemies were not the brutal and the depraved but the very men he pitied, the men he wanted to help."[58] The Assistant Commissioner has no faith like Caroline Bury, no belief in a great directing purpose in a world where there is so much suffering and injustice. His only answer is resignation to the work. He seeks to shelve his troubled conscience by the idea of loyalty to the system which he serves. But the conflict between his humanity and the desire to be on the right side is overwhelming. His "sense of a great waste, a useless expenditure of lives"[59] shakes his mind and he is half-inclined to resign. But soon his spirits rise when he begins to write comments on the Streatham report. He quickly puts out of his mind the thought of resigning as soon as he recalls the satisfaction his job gives him: ". . . his spirits rose; all that worried him dropped away. . . he began to write . . . It was for these moments of unsought revelation that the Assistant Commissioner lived."[60] Despite the absence of rational justification, he resigns himself to work and seems to be coming close to the "absurd man". The mythic symbol of this man, according to Albert Camus, is Sisyphus, who, despite his being condemned "to ceaselessly rolling a rock to the top of a mountain, whence the stone would fall back of its own weight",[61] not only endures but also finds joy in his task.

The characters of the present novel represent man suffering from alienation and isolation in modern life in which emphasis is on standardization and conformity at the loss of man's individuality. An individual feels lost and powerless in the world. Greene examines the nature of man's existence in light of progress made in the field of science and technology and points out that the present industrialized life has a dehumanizing influence on the individual. The chaos and disorder the novel emphasizes are not merely the characteristics of modern life, but they convey a strong sense of meaninglessness of human existence in general.

England Made Me, like *The Man Within* and *It's a Battlefield*, is concerned with man's alienation arising out of modern capitalism. Here Greene presents a world solely governed by economic interests and, like the existentialists, criticizes the modern tendency to devitalize man. He points out that the industrial system, which increased the sources of man's pleasure and comfort, dispossessed man of himself.

Krogh, an expatriate, is a megalomaniac Swedish Financier, who lives, surrounded by himself, in a large office-building. The initials of his name flashing at him in the electric lights, that adorn every doorway of his office, give him immense pleasure. The richest man of the world, Krogh, risen to this state from the humblest beginning of a peasant born in a wooden cottage, is proud of the vast dividends and new flotations he has created by his own efforts. A man "made of money"[62] and slave to his fortune, Krogh is always occupied with the thought of profit and loss and is "tied to the end of a phone. Money, figures, shares, morning till night".[63] He is very happy while dealing with figures: ". . . there was nothing he didn't know about figures, there was nothing he couldn't do with them, there was nothing human about them."[64] He adopts all means, fair and foul, to improve his property, and his rapacious greed for wealth dehumanizes him. In his business deals he has no regard for human and moral considerations. He tells lies and practises frauds and frame-ups to increase his financial power. What is fraud for others, is "clarity" for him. A fraud carried out successfully, fills him with "a pure inhuman joy". His financial power and astuteness destroy the power of his judgment. He is irritated at his inability to appreciate a work of art. The absence of feeling for it makes him feel uneasy: ". . . no instinct told him whether it was good art or bad art; he did not understand. He was uneasy, but he did not show his uneasiness."[65]

He lacks both time and energy to enjoy poetry and music though he is unwilling to admit it. He adopts an expert's opinion on a work of art as his own. In the opera he sits with an empty seat on either hand so that he may not be seen dozing. His alienation from the past is indicated by the fact that he and his friend Hall address each other as Mr. and Hall: "They had once spoken on such level terms that they had been Jim and Erik (not Hall and Mr. Krogh), borrowing each other's boiler-suit, drinking together at the wine shop."[66] Ill at ease with men, he shuns contact with them as much as he can. He reflects on his total failure in human relationship: "One could not plan a human relationship like a graph of production. He tried to encourage himself. . . I have been too taken up by finance, I must enlarge my scope—the human side."[67]

His covetousness turns him into a brute. Incapable of love and his senses being almost dead, he feels no pity for poor Anderson and throws him out of his job craftily. He feels guilty and restless and declines to see young Anderson seeking an interview. Marriage has lost its usual meaning. He is willing to marry Kate just for a business settlement. This marriage will prevent Kate from leaking out his illegal business secrets. Kate comments: "Perhaps this is what Erik feels, this sense of a sum solved, the square root taken, the logarithm correctly read."[68] Krogh is an extremely self-conscious man. In spite of his financial success, he always feels restless. Like Kate, Anthony and Minty, he too is fighting for his own security. He is not the future, he is not self-sufficient, rather he is one, like others, "out of his proper place".[69] Though a self-made business magnate, he is as displaced as Anthony and Minty and after twenty years of prosperity, he is still uneasy, still afraid of a slip in manner which would betray his peasant birth. Though his wealth can purchase everything for him, Krogh is always troubled by "a sense of something lost, neglected, stubbornly alive[70] because it cannot purchase for him real happiness and felicity of soul.

Hall, an Englishman and a former friend, and now Krogh's henchman, is another dehumanized figure in the novel. He possesses no quality "but obedience to the man who paid him, fidelity to the man he admired".[71] His loyalty to Krogh is evident from the way he cruelly strikes Anderson and feels no pity for the young boy heaving himself on to his knees with his face dripping blood, mouth and eyes full of blood: "Hall felt no anger against him, no sympathy, only a deep unselfish love for Krogh which had no relation to the money he was paid."[72] He mercilessly pushes Anthony into the lake for Krogh. Thus he is the malevolent and destructive agent of modern capitalism, the embodiment of cruelty and violence.

Kate Farrant, Krogh's secretary and mistress and Anthony's twin-sister in many ways, is a foil to her brother. She adapts herself to the situation in which she is placed whereas Anthony is a total failure. Anthony is lost in the world of "business that she knew so well, the world she knew so well".[73] Though full of hatred for Krogh, who thinks in figures and who does not feel vague things about people, she agrees to marry him only to safeguard herself and her brother whom she is unwilling to lose: "We're done, we are broke, we belong to the past, we haven't the character or the energy to do more than hang on to something new for what we can make out of it. Krogh is worth us both."[74] Anthony protests, Kate on the other hand desperately conforms to the new values.

Minty, the little dusty man, is probably the most pitiable of all the exiles in the novel. The first of Greene's full length grotesques, he earns his living by reporting on Krogh, who is news. He does not drink and has an ascetic contempt for women. He, like Conder the newspaper man in *It's a Battlefield,* is a man without hopes and ambitions and lives all alone in his attic room with the Harrow photographs, "the missal in the cupboard,... the spider withering under the glass, a home from home".[75] Like the spider that symbolizes his existence. Minty is truly trapped and he clings to his wretched loneliness. Anxious to make friends, he marks the reflection of his own seediness in Anthony and befriends him. But Anthony is killed and he is destined to live alone.

Anthony Farrant is the best character in the novel because in drawing him, Greene has depended on his imagination. There is something of Greene himself in him. Other characters seem to be made by his intellect, they conform to a system whereas Anthony by his very nature can conform to no scheme. He has boasted, lied and cheated his way through jobs all over the world. He wears school colours to which he is not entitled and talks an argot which is a strain on the reader's patience. He is doomed in the new situation and has a sense of not having "a future".[76] He is unreliable, deceitful in small ways and hopeless with money. He seems to be an example of what E.M. Forster called "the undeveloped heart". Kate thinks that he is "too innocent to live".[77] His failure and weakness, as it is clear from the text, are related to his childhood. His depraved innocence "has its roots in his Berkhemsted school days".[78] He remembers the unhappy experiences of school life: "This was victory; somehow to have existed; happiness was an incidental enjoyment;... It was perhaps the only lesson he had thoroughly learned at school, the lesson taught by the thirteen weeks of overcrowding, tedium and fear. Somehow time passed and the worst came to an end."[79]

He thus reminds us of Greene's own feeling of boredom at school. It is indicated that Anthony's future was determined in his childhood and his father with his maxims of chastity, prudence and honesty did a great damage to him. Kate recalls "he loved Anthony and ruined Anthony".[80] Though he has been a victim of his situation, he has scope to exercise his free will and transcend his surroundings. To a great extent he is responsible for what he is and has gone wrong on account of his own innate character. He displays his unwillingness to give in to external pressure. He is sick of precepts: "Lectures, my God, how many lectures in a man's life? ... I'm Anthony Farrant as good as they are."[81] He is the free individual, anxious to be his own self. "He was quiet, he was sincere, he was completely himself."[82] His conscience, supine for some time, is stirred at the end, and out of a sense of fair play he defies the order of his employer to throw out young Anderson. He replies, "I'm dammed if I will."[83] He thus speaks out his mind and challenges the authority of Krogh. Terribly disgusted with the place, unable to conform to the new existence despite the riches and social importance he enjoyed while serving with Krogh, he gives up his job and leaves for home: "I'm tired of this place," Anthony says, "No room for push, initiative."[84] So it may be said that Anthony is a social product, the living criticism of a system. He is also a man who is produced by shiftless nature in no matter what environment. He is an incarnation of natural spontaneous human weakness.

Here Greene has created a world that is chaotic and irrational. It is a world of absurdity where nothing turns out as it should. Kate's plan for Anthony's security is not materialized. Anthony's desire to make Krogh human is also rendered futile. Characters drawn here are alienated from themselves as well as from others. Krogh, Hall, Kate, Minty, Anthony are all exiled, Minty is one of those who have no vigour to resist this world: "They were neither one thing nor the other; they were really only happy when they were together. . . ."[85] With a deep sense of disappointment Minty utters, "Every one goes, only Minty stays."[86] Kate is also unhappy about this world and moves on to another exile leaving behind Krogh and Hall bound together in a terrible isolation: "They had nothing to say to each other, what lay between them, held them apart, left them lonely."[87]

Anthony alone insists upon maintaining his unique consciousness in the face of the overwhelming pressures to conform. Graham Greene denounces materialistic progress that has corrupted and destroyed the individuality of men. He comes very close to Marcel who is a bitter critic of the present-day acquisitive society. Marcel looks upon "having" as a source of alienation. "To have" means to be able to dispose of. It also leads to being dispossessed. So "having" is also girt about by the fear of loss. Those who have are in a state of tension and those who have not are in a state of resentment. Greene's characters exemplify this view. Krogh is as much a prisoner of his fortune as others are the victims of their poverty. But the alienating factor is also in man's own temperament. Greene sees man a free moral agent who is paradoxically free to choose his actions. Because of this freedom to choose, responsibility is inescapable. This view places Greene in the company of the existentialists.

This brief survey of Greene's three important early novels leads us to conclude that his main concern in these novels is contemporary man's alienation. The alienating factor is in the environment as well as in man's own temperament. In *The Man Within*, the alienating factor is parental pressure and lack of integrated education. The protagonist attains self-discovery through terror and love. *It's a Battlefield* shows the alienating effects of red tape, bureaucracy and capitalism and communicates a sense of the meaninglessness of life. Greene diagnoses the illness of modern man but suggests no way out of it. Characters are deprived of spiritual consolation which Andrews has though for a very short while. *England Made Me* criticizes the present commercial civilization which has ravaged human spirit and reduced man to the status of an object like other objects in nature or, to use Martin Buber's term, a manipulable "It", Sartre's *L'ensoi* or the "in-itself". Stripped of his subjectivity (his thouness) man is alienated from his authentic self. Greene's early novels, like Camus's *The Stranger* and Kafka's *The Castle*, give a vivid picture of a man who is a stranger in his world, a stranger to other people whom he pretends to love. He moves about in a state of homelessness as if he were in a foreign country where he does not know the language and has no hope of learning it, but is always doomed to wander in quiet despair, incommunicado, home-ess and a stranger.

Notes and References

1. Leslie Paul, *The Meaning of Human Existence* (London: Faber and Faber Ltd., 1949), p. 221.
2. Graham Greene, *The Man Within* (London: William Heinemann Ltd., 1929), Penguin Books, 1971, p. 24.

3. *Ibid.* 4. *Ibid.*, p. 17. 5. *Ibid.*, p. 25.
6. *Ibid.*, p. 37. 7. *Ibid.*, p. 169. 8. *Ibid.*, p. 52.
9. *Ibid.*, p. 174. 10. *Ibid.*, p. 139. 11. *Ibid.*, p. 56.
12. *Ibid.*, p. 193. 13. *Ibid.*, p. 166. 14. *Ibid.*, p. 167.
15. *Ibid.* 16. *Ibid.*, p. 220.

17. Colin Wilson, *The Outsider* (London: Pan Books Ltd., 1956), p. 316.
18. *The Man Within*, p. 75.

19. *Ibid.*, p. 69. 20. *Ibid.*, p. 214. 21. *Ibid.*, pp. 169-70.

22. One of the most curious characteristics of human beings—particularly Westerners—is that pain and inconvenience stimulate their vitality far more than pleasure." *Beyond the Outsider*, p. 31.
23. Quoted in Greene's *It's a Battlefield* (London: William Heinemann Ltd., 1934), Penguin Books, 1971, p. 6.
24. "Joseph Conrad's *The Secret Agent* and Graham Greene's *Its a Battlefield*: A Study in Structural Meaning", *Modern Fiction Studies*, No. 2, XVI (Summer 1970), p. 123.
25. *It's a Battlefield*, p. 71.

26. *Ibid.*, p. 9. 27. *Ibid*, p. 29. 28. *Ibid.*, p. 150.

29. Atkins, *Graham Greene*, pp. 42-3.
30. *It's a Battlefield*, p. 58.

31. *Ibid.*, p. 188. 32. *Ibid.*, p. 133. 33. *Ibid.*, p. 44.
34. *Ibid.*, p. 39. 35. *Ibid.*, p. 27. 36. *Ibid.*, p. 29.
37. *Ibid.*, p. 58. 38. *Ibid.*, p. 150. 39. *Ibid.*, p. 70.
40. *Ibid.*, p. 67. 41. *Ibid.*, p. 68. 42. *Ibid.*, p. 64.
43 *Ibid.* 44. *Ibid.*, pp. 32-3. 45. *Ibid.*, p. 118.

46. *Ibid.*, p. 126.
47. "The rebel is a slave who has taken orders all his life, suddenly decides that he cannot obey some new command."

A. Camus, *The Rebel,* trans. A. Bower (London: Hamish Hamilton, 1956), Penguin Books, 1973, p. 19.

48. A.A. Devitis, *Graham Greene* (New York: Twayne Publishers, 1964), p. 73.
49. *It's a Battlefield,* p. 189.
50. *Ibid.*, p. 190. 51. *Ibid.*, p. 192.
52. A. Camus, *The Myth of Sisyphus,* trans. Justin O'Brien (London: Hamish Hamilton, 1955), Penguin Books, 1977, p. 43.
53. *It's a Battlefield,* p. 13.
54. *Ibid.*, p. 73. 55. *Ibid.*, p.184. 56. *Ibid.*, p. 81.
57. J. Conrad, *Lord Jim* (J.M. Dent and Sons, 1900), Penguin Books, 1976, p. 14.
58. *It's a Battlefield,* p. 165.
59. *Ibid.*, p. 191. 60. *Ibid.*, p. 202.
61. *The Myth of Sisyphus,* p. 107.
62. Graham Greene, *England Made Me* (London: William Heinemann Ltd., 1935), Penguin Books, 1974, p. 116.
63. *Ibid* , p. 44 64. *Ibid.*, p. 131. 65. *Ibid.*, p. 34.
66. *Ibid.*, p. 43. 67. *Ibid.*, p. 49. 68. *Ibid.*, p. 142.
69. *Ibid.*, p. 158. 70. *Ibid.*, p. 39. 71. *Ibid.*, p. 162.
72. *Ibid.*, p. 176. 73. *Ibid.*, p. 11. 74. *Ibid.*, p. 135.
75. *Ibid.*, p. 207. 76. *Ibid.*, p. 29. 77. *Ibid.*, p. 186.
78. K. Allott and M. Farris, *The Art of Graham Greene* (London: Hamish Hamilton, 1951), p. 108.
79. *England Made Me,* p. 51. 80. *Ibid.*, p. 64.
81. *Ibid.*, p. 19. 82. *Ibid.*, p. 29. 83. *Ibid.*, p. 174.
84. *Ibid.*, p. 183. 85. *Ibid.*, p. 180. 86. *Ibid.*, p. 181.
87. *Ibid.*, p. 205.

CHAPTER TWO

The Existential Christian

GRAHAM GREENE'S religious novels echo the themes of alienation, anxiety and the existential relation between man and God which have been emphatically treated by the Christian existentialists: Kierkegaard, Marcel, Jaspers, Buber and Tillich. A brief account of the views of these existentialists with regard to man's alienation, "sickness unto death" and "leap of faith" will be helpful in tracing a similarity between Greene and the existentialists and his intellectual dependence upon them.

The Christian existentialists, like their atheistic counterparts, are repelled by the mass-man to which human beings have been reduced by various forms of totalitarian Government and by the very characteristics of industrial society which we usually count as a mark of progress. They criticize all dehumanizing forms of collectivism and stress the individual's need to extricate himself from the crowd in order to be fully himself. Kierkegaard has little use for the "crowd" or the "public" and summons the individual to come out from the crowd and take the burden of his being upon himself: "A crowd in its very concept is the untruth, by reason of the fact that it renders the individual completely impenitent and irresponsible or at least weakens his sense of responsibility by reducing it to a fraction."[1] Heidegger's expression for the crowd is "they"[2] (das man). The "they" takes away choice, disburdens the individual of his responsibility, determines standards of tastes and morals. Karl Jaspers uses the expression "mass-existence" or the *mass*[3] to indicate the domination of life and standards by the unthinking multitude. He sees this danger as one that is prevalent to a peculiar degree in the close living conditions of the modern industrialized and urbanized state, especially in his book *Man in the Modern Age*. Marcel is the relentless critic of the "functional man". The "functional man", reduced to a factor in the empirical social reality, is deprived of mystery, dignity, personhood, and eventually of humanity itself. Man is not merely a "functional man", he is better described as *homo-viator*.[4]

These existentialists rebel against too much emphasis on scientific rationalism in our time and point out that contemporary disorder has grown in the face of what is known, what is planned and what is understood to be rational. Existence is a paradox which cannot be neatly understood by rational thought. There is no rational or human solution to the dilemma of existence. Marcel observes: "... the intelligence has no grasp on reality... Existence, properly speaking, is incapable of characterization... the mind when confronting it cannot adopt without contradiction the attitude that is needed for characterizing something."[5] According to Martin Buber, "This is the glorious paradox of our existence that all comprehensibility of the world is only a footstool of its incomprehensibility."[6] These existentialists distrust reason and plead for an acceptance of the presence of wonder, mystery and the irrational in life.

In advanced modern societies man is essentially alienated because he has come under the possession of a number of mechanisms beyond his understanding and control. No longer the master of his own life, man suffers from a sense of powerlessness, abandonment and indifference. He is angst-ridden and has neither desire nor zest for life.

Kierkegaard associates anxiety with man's peculiar constitution as body and soul, established in spirit. In the very way he is constituted, man is subject to a tension and, this tension is despair, the "sickness unto death". Kierkegaard discusses the theme of despair at some length in his book *Sickness Unto Death.* Kierkegaard observes: "The Despair which is conscious of being Despair, as also it is Conscious of being a Self wherein there is after all something Eternal, and then is either in despair at not willing to be itself, or in despair at willing to be itself."[7] This despair can take any one of these forms: despair at not willing to be one self, or despair at not willing to be a self, despair at willing to be another than one self wishing for a new self. The immediate man helps himself in a different way, he wishes to be another. The immediate man does not recognize his self, he recognizes that he has a self only by externals. Kierkegaard assigns a positive role to despair as a propaedeutic to faith. To endure anxiety is to have one's eyes opened to the reality of the human condition.

The inefficacy of technics, the impotence of individual effort against totalitarianism and the anonymity to which industrialism condemns the individual—all induce despair. Marcel's reaction to all this is contained especially in his short book, *The Philosophy of Existence*, and in *Homo Viator*. Despair, he says, is an expression of "the will to 'negation' as applied to being."[8] Despair is the discovery not only of a flawed world but of a completely broken one. Hope and despair, however, are correlated. The possibility of unconquerable hope lies only in a world of despair: "The truth is that there can, strictly speaking, be no hope except when the temptation to despair exists. Hope is the act by which this temptation is actively or victoriously overcome."[9] Hope is looked on as a virtue by Marcel. It is both an ethical and a religious category: "As an ethical category it has affinity with patience, with relaxation."[10] As a religious category it is inseparable from faith, a self-abandonment in absolute confidence. To hope is to be the very reverse of being isolated. Despair is connected with isolation, hope with the bonds of communion.

The theme of anxiety appears in Karl Jaspers too. He points out that life seems to have grown "indefinitely vast;"[11] it no longer has that "interlinkage"[12] which holds it together so that it is not frittered away. A man has the function that he performs for eight hours a day, and he has his bit of breathing-space somewhere in the urban or suburban wilderness. Jaspers writes: "What is new about this age. . . is that man becomes conscious of being as a whole, of himself and his limitations. He experiences the terror of the world, and his own powerlessness. He asks radical questions. Face to face with the void, he strives for liberation and redemption. By consciously recognizing his limits, he sets himself the highest goals. He experiences absoluteness in the depths of selfhood and in the lucidity of transcendence."[13]

Paul Tillich has treated the theme of anxiety in his book *The Courage to Be*. He points out that "Man is drawn into the world of objects and has lost his subjectivity in it. But he is still aware of what he has lost or is continuously losing. He is still man enough to experience his dehumanization as despair."[14]

Like atheistic existentialists, Christian existentialists too are rebels who struggle against the accepted authorities and the traditional canons of the organized religion. The atheistic existentialists say that only after the total denial of conventional beliefs and standards can new possibilities arise and a transvaluation of values take place. In a similar manner, the Christian existentialists are sometimes in total revolt against the traditional forms of faith. They claim that only through the rejection and denial of these forms and through the consequent painful experience of having nothing left can new faith arise. For the Christian, too, there can be a radical transvaluation, not far removed from the experience of the nihilist.

Kierkegaard's teaching about the three stages of life is elaborated in his *Either/Or*, *Stages on Life's Way* and *The Concluding Unscientific Postsript*. The three stages—an aesthetic, an ethical and a religious which are comparable to the Hindu "*Ashramas*"—are ways of life, modes of existing. These stages are: "not distinguished abstractly, as the immediate mediate and the synthesis of the two but rather concretely, in existential determinations, as enjoyment-perdition, action-victory; suffering."[15] The stages are not really stages but progressive deepenings of life, in which what went before is taken up into a richer texture. Aestheticism is at the base of the existential scale. The aesthete is someone who chooses to live for the happiness of the moment. But the aesthetic attitude in the end lapses into boredom, disgust and despair. The aesthete is driven into a panicky flight from the prospect of boredom, and this flight, which is a flight from himself, becomes his form of desperation and therefore of despair. The ethical man chooses himself and his life, resolutely and consciously in the face of death. Such a course is accomplished by a "leap", by a complete break with the aesthetic way of life. In the religious sphere of existence, the individual is called upon to go beyond the ethical and he does so in fear and trembling and not in the callous arrogance of power. The individual can transcend the universally recognized principles of morality by virtue of what Kierkegaard calls "teleological suspension of ethics."[16] Kierkegaard's aim was to find his reader on the aesthetic level and lead him on to the highest form of existence—the religious, specifically the life of the Christian faith. In his *Attack Upon Christendom*, he criticizes official Christianity and explains quite convincingly what is meant by becoming a true Christian. To Kierkegaard, Christianity aims at "a total transformation in a man".[17] One is not a Christian by prayer, baptism or confession. "Christianity is precisely an affair of spirit and so of subjectivity and so of inwardness."[18] We are reminded of Hamlet to whom existence and non-existence have only subjective significance: "There is nothing either good or bad, but thinking make it so."[19] Knowledge of God is an inward experience. "God is a subject, and therefore exists only for subjectivity in inwardness."[20] Modesty is the hallmark of spirituality. Kierkegaard's spiritual man is free from himself and from his passion. He achieves the experience of the transcendence of human existence by the act of transcending himself. He comes very close to the ideal of the "Sthita Prajna" of the *Bhagvad-Gita*.

The sudden "leap", through which everything is changed, is the fundamental tenet of Christian existential philosophy. Faith means complete surrender. Self-knowledge is more relevant to faith than reason. To make movements of faith one must shut one's eyes and plunge confidently into the absurd and take the risk of jumping into the abyss. He approaches God in fear and trembling as does Kierkegaard's Abraham Kierkegaard observes: "Without risk there is no faith. Faith is precisely the contradiction between the infinite passion of the individual's inwardness and the objective uncertainty."[21] Marcel too, who found the austere moral gloomy ethos of nineteenth-century rationalism stifling and uncongenial, insists on the inefficiency of the rational proofs of the existence of God and the significance of the blind intuition which powerfully promotes hope and faith. He says: "Faith needs to triumph over the state of self-division which is bound up with the conditions of existence of a finite being."[22]

His *Metaphysical Journal* is full of insights into the connection between human and divine love. For Marcel, as for Buber, the divine "Thou" and the human "Thou" are, as it were, avenues to each other. Loving and suffering are deeply related and this is the inner meaning of *agape*, the descending movement of love. According to Marcel, ". . . to love someone truly is to love him in God,"[23] God the absolute "Thou", who can never become a "Him". "To pray is actively to refuse to think God as order, it is to think him as really God, as pure Thou."[24] Martin Buber too insists on the "I-Thou" relationship with God because the relation to the "Thou" is direct: "No system of ideas, no fore-knowledge, and no fancy intervene between 'I' and 'Thou'. The memory itself is transformed, as it plunges out of isolation into the unity of the whole. No aim, no test and no anticipation intervene between 'I' and 'Thou'."[25] According to Paul Tillich, faith is the courage of despair. It is not a place where one can live, it is without the safety of words and concepts, it is without a name, a church, a cult, a theology. Faith comprises both itself and the doubt of itself. He remarks: "Living faith includes the doubt about itself, the courage to take this doubt into itself, and the risk of courage."[26]

Thus faith is an attitude of trust and commitment in mystery. Though faith goes beyond what is known, it is not arbitrary nor its way of taking the world is totally unfounded. Faith takes its rise from some insight. The experience of human love is a prerequisite for the realization of divine love. It becomes real love only in the world, in relation to the individual human being and it develops into enthusiasm for the beauty of existence. Jaspers aptly observes: "Love without the world is love of nothing, a groundless bliss. Love of Transcendence is real only as loving transfiguration of the world."[27] Thus the Christian existentialists make effort to restore a reverential love of the created. The Christianity they emphasize is first and last a Christian humanism.

The themes of alienation and anxiety, which appeared in Greene's early novels, receive more emphatic treatment in his *Brighton Rock*. Moreover, the novel introduces Greene's concern with man's freedom of faith and his impatience with the church and its rituals.

The novel offers an interesting picture of the crisis in Western civilization. Graham Greene is acquainted with the rational outlook of our time which suggests that economic and environmental factors determine the behaviour of the individual and which believes in the improvement of life through various social institutions. Ida Arnold observes, "Man is made by the places in which he lives."[28] Pinkie is seized with a bitter feeling of nausea to remember his indifferent parents and the ugly environment of his early childhood and, like Andrews of *The Man Within*, thinks that he is what his parents have made him. Pinkie complains against his childhood, "hell lay about him in his infancy."[29] But Greene does not believe in the compulsive nature of the situation and points out that human beings are unique and their behaviour is independent of environment. Aliénation is a moral category and there is no alienating situation in itself. A man may live out his condition as one that alienates whereas another in the same position may not experience it. Some are well adapted and do not feel truncated or alienated. Rose and Pinkie illustrate this point. Exposed to similar influences, raised in the same neighbourhood of Brighton by similarly disinterested parents, they react differently. Rose transcends the values that shape Pinkie. Like the existentialists, Greene stresses that all men's alibis are unacceptable. No God, no environment, no heredity is responsible for his character, man stands alone in the universe, responsible for his condition.

Greene, like the existentialists, tends to despise conventional morality and insists on the significance of man's obedience to the deeper level of conscience. The term "conscience" is somewhat ambiguous. It may mean a person's awareness of the moral code accepted in his society. It also stands for an individual's conviction that transcends the accepted standard of his society. Existentialists are critical of the conscience in the first sense and hold that only the second is important. The clash between the two levels of conscience is dramatically presented by Kierkegaard in his story of Abraham and Issac in the book *Fear and Trembling*. Abraham is ready to go against moral principles and his human feelings to obey God's command. He is ready to set aside the "universal", that is to say, the generally accepted standard of what is right, in order to carry out the duty uniquely laid on him as the individual before God. In Heidegger, the conventional moral obligation is known as "public conscience", the voice of the "they" which simply reflects the commonly accepted standards of right and wrong. The true conscience functions precisely in delivering us from the voice of the "they": "Conscience summons Dasein's self from its lostness in the 'they'."[30] The *Dasein* can truly hear the call of conscience, the call that comes from the depth of one's own being, only when he stops listening to the voice of the "they".

The theme of basic confrontation of the two levels of existence, the spiritual and the earthly, that the novel presents most clearly, seems to have a close affinity with the theme of different levels of conscience in existentialist philosophy. Rose, who understands that she and Pinkie are of the realm of good and evil and are on a different level with values different from those of the world of right and wrong which Ida and all the others inhabit, articulates this basic confrontation: "It's her . . . Asking questions. Soft as butter. What does she know about us? . . . She does not know what a mortal sin is . . . Right and wrong. That's what she talks about."[31] Pinkie, who in material terms has been nowhere and has done nothing, has more grasp of reality than the engaging and well-covered woman, learned in the ways of the world and the appetite and comforts of the flesh. "She is just nothing",[32] Pinkie thinks. Ida, who represents middle-class materialism, common in the modern world, is full of vitality and is quite sure that life is worth living: "Ida Arnold was on the right side, she was cheery, she was healthy . . . She was honest, she was kindly, she belonged to the great middle law-abiding class."[33]

She knows what is right and what is wrong and the mission of her life is to right the wrong and see that evil is duly punished. She strives for justice, "an eye for an eye", law and order. Right and wrong, the big vague abstractions which provide Ida spiritual sustenance, are anathema to Rose and Pinkie. Her ruthless pursuit of Pinkie results in another murder and suicide and it is suggested that Ida's optimism is dangerous and remorseless. Pinkie's devotion to sin and Rose's participation as the part of a bargain are set on a higher level than Ida's decency and generosity. Greene seems to be of the view that anything on the higher level is superior to anything on the lower level. Thus the situation of the novel—Rose and Pinkie having similar upbringing but choosing different values, evil needing "goodness"[34] and degradation of Ida representing conventional norms—seems to be remotely derived from Camus and Kafka and certifies Greene's denunciation of the rational and his leaning towards the irrational and incongruous in life.

The experience of angst, that is a characteristic aspect of modern temperament, is a prominent theme of the novel. Pinkie's friends—Cubitt, Spricer and Dallow—are loyal to the gang and are unaware of having a self. They are "immediate men" who do not recognize their selves and who are merely concerned with earning their livelihood. Ida too is a slave to the traditional ideal of justice and is ignorant of any despair of not having a self. Mr. Colleoni, a rich business man, is lost in the superficial glamour of life: "The visible world was all Mr. Colleoni's."[35] Rose and Pinkie, on the other hand, are conscious of "sickness unto death". Though Rose decides to marry Pinkie in full "knowledge"[36] of his wickedness as her encounters with Ida and her existential encounter with Pinkie reveal, her decision is anxiety-ridden. In spite of her awareness of Pinkie's life, Rose is always full of hope that Pinkie will change. She is pleading with Ida, "People change",[37] Pinkie may not be past all hope. She believes in the eventuality of good and evil, "Nothing was decided—there was always hope."[38] The frustration of her expectations, as Pinkie never changes, stirs a terrible feeling of anxiety in Rose. Pinkie too, like Rose, is conscious that existence is "sickness unto death". Pinkie's feeling of anxiety is not an inner conflict nor does it result from his breach of duty, rather it lies at the root of his alienation from society through his criminality as well as his self-estrangement that involves an anxious longing for the lost ideal and his awareness of the absurd in life. His conscious efforts to escape the horror of his childhood—a knowledge of poverty, hate and premature experience of sex—the "game" leading man to "the stuffy room, the wakeful children, the Saturday night movements from the other bed... worth murdering a world"[39] through asceticism—no drink, no cigarettes, no woman—"To marry—it was like ordure on hands"[40] and through his dedication to "Credo in unum Satanum"[41] do not materialize. Rose brings him back to his own past and Piker, a thin undernourished boy like himself, rises from the past to remind him of a smoky childhood, "a cracked bell ringing, a child weeping under the cane".[42] Pinkie's anxiety for the lost ideal is more painful than the unsuccessful attempt to escape his past. The whole lost world moves in his spoilt voice when he repeats the words of the liturgy: "Angus Dei, quitoll is peccata mundi, dona nobis pacem."[43] Pinkie longs for peace but there is to be no peace for him. "Heaven" is just a word and he cannot believe in its peace: "Hell was something he could trust. A brain was only capable of what it could conceive and it could not conceive what it had never experienced."[44]

Moreover, the experience of the absurd augments his feeling of anxiety. The painful feeling of not being able to deal with his special situation also implies the anxiety about human situation. He feels that life is ugly and painful, it is "hell"[45] and no one is out of it: "It's jail, it's not knowing where to get money. Worms and cataract, cancer. You hear 'em shrieking from the upper windows—children being born. It's dying slowly."[46] Life is full of confusions, contradictions and incongruities. It is ambiguous and incalculable. Pinkie sees life as a series of complicated tactical exercises, as complicated as the alignments at Waterloo."[47]

Greene, like the Christian existentialists, assigns a positive role to anxiety. The experience of angst is prelusive to faith. Greene points out that the man enduring anxiety becomes aware of the reality of the human situation. Rose in the present novel reveals "the courage of despair", *i.e.* the courage to affirm humanity despite everything problematic and uncertain. In spite of all nihilism in modern literature, hope and faith springing from the courage of despair constitute the distinguishing mark of the modern hero. Though shaken by an awful doubt to detect Pinkie's sexual repulsion and his instinctive withdrawal from her in the country-drive, Rose does not abandon hope for the future. It is enough that she loves: "It didn't matter; she loves him; she had her responsibility."[48]

Her responsibility in love is the basis of her willingness to suffer damnation with Pinkie. This forms the nucleus of the novel, its fundamental affirmation. During the final death-ride, Rose is torn between her loyalty to her pledge and her conscience that reminds her of her autonomous existence and she trembles inside but never loses trust in herself. Like Kierkegaard's Abraham, she teleologically suspends all ethical considerations and enters the narrow path of faith, having no one to understand her situation and give her counsel. It comes like a revelation as if someone has whispered to her that she is some one, a separate creature, not just one flesh with him and "she could always escape".[49] Hearing Pinkie's name shouted through the rain in wilderness, Rose puts down the revolver and escapes the deadly plan as she feels, "this must mean good news."[50] After the death of Pinkie, Rose finds herself in the most adverse moment of her life. She, however, reveals the "courage to be" and moves beyond the adversity of the immediate situation. With the sudden conviction that she carries life, a feeling of immense gratitude breaks through the pain and Rose gets the "sight a long way off of life going on again"[51] and walks to face "the worst horror of all",[52] the revelation that the phonograph record holds for her. But this wouldn't destroy her as she has faced unexpected facts before.

Rose's capacity to receive the unexpected as an occasion for hope implies some kind of "leap", a leap beyond the immediate situation. Pinkie's feeling of anxiety too takes on a religious meaning and, just by a sudden leap, he can also rise to the higher religious level: "An enormous emotion beat on him, it was like something trying to get in... Dona nobis pacem."[53] The light of God approaching him through Rose can redeem him, but a positive response means a total surrender of his self and the scarifice of the governing principle of his personality. He is filled with a terrible feeling of resentment for not having his chance and seeing "his glimpse of heaven if it was only a crack between the Brighton walls...".[54] But he resists the glimpses of heaven getting to him through Rose with concentrated hatred and fear bred from the pain and treachery and squalor of his life and asserts his individuality. Though no longer a legal witness to his crime, Rose is a witness to his inwardness and even her humility seems to be a trap to him. Her boundless love, unshaken by the knowledge of his evil, is a terrible shock to him. He plans to eliminate her so that "he would be free again nothing to think about but himself, Myself".[55] On failing to respond dynamically to the faint inner voice which tells him of his weakness and calls him back to another way of life, Pinkie sets about his end. Tormented by anxiety, Pinkie falls a victim to despair and involves himself in a process of self-destruction.

Graham Greene, like the Christian existentialists, protests against the perversion of Christianity by Christian institutions and refuses the ministration of the church. The present novel condemns traditional forms of faith and shows the significance of faith based on man's free will. Though a Roman Catholic, Rose commits the mortal sin by marrying without sacraments. The idea of hell does not deter her: "If they damn him, they have got to damn her too."[56] She watches the people coming back from mass and feels no envy for them: "They had their salvation and she had Pinkie and damnation."[57] With the possibilities of hope for the change of Pinkie exhausted, her impulses of the Catholic training urge her to recant by an axiom as an alternative to existential commitment: "You can plead for him at the throne of grace,"[58] but she does not allow self-deception to buttress her passion to survive. It is death not damnation that scares her. Like Rose, Pinkie too is full of hatred for the sacraments. Though he feels "a faint nostalgia for the tiny dark confessional box",[59] something he has lost or forgotten or rejected, hearing the faint call of God rising from the depth of his conscience, he is not ready for confession, penance and the sacrament as all this will be "an awful distraction".[60] Unable to bear the pressure of existence here and now, Pinkie kills himself and thus commits the most serious crime to a Roman Catholic who believes in "hell and its fire". His death destroying his "existence"[61] here and now speaks of the significance of the worldly life. Rose's relation to Pinkie and her choice of life without hope and of world without end for the child who is growing within her, speak of the importance of human suffering in this world. The novel expresses Greene's indignation with the priests who, instead of understanding the real problem of the penitent and asking him to be true to his ownself, talk of rules and God's mercy. The priest, who comments on the "appalling strangeness of the mercy of God"[62] and asks Rose to "hope and pray",[63] reminds us of the elder of Dostoyevsky's *The Brothers Karamazov,* I, to whom God's love is "inconceivable".[64] Rose does not know how to hope and pray. Without following the rules of the church, she attains spirituality through her love and becomes the existential advocate of churchless Christianity.

Thus in *Brighton Rock*, Greene emphasizes, like the Christian existentialists, the themes of alienation, anxiety, "leap of faith" and human suffering; he criticizes modern emphasis on narrow rationalism and points out the irrelevance of church and its rules to true faith.

The Power and the Glory, like its predecessor, *Brighton Rock*, criticizes the dehumanizing elements in modern life, shows the importance of faith rising from man's personal experience and human affliction and points out the irrelevance of the doctrines and ceremonies of the conventional church. Greene is critical of the modern narrowly rationalistic belief in social utopia and pleads for an acceptance of the wonder and the mystery of the irrational in life. The strength of the present novel is based on an interesting contrast between the materialistic and the spiritual approach to life. The Lieutenant is a staunch rationalist, who holds a purely materialistic view of life and is fanatically opposed to the church for its insistence on the unimportance of human lot in this world. The Lieutenant is the direct opponent of the Priest as Ida is Pinkie's. Having no taste for music, art and religion, the Lieutenant lives in a room "as comfortless as a prison or a monastic cell".[65] It infuriates him to think that there are still people in the State who believe in a loving and merciful God. He is firmly determined to wipe out everything which reminds him of his miserable childhood. He wants "to destroy everything: to be alone without any memories at all".[66] A modern Prometheus, with a devotion only to the reality of the here and now, he is in revolt against pain, misery and oppression of the people and wants to drive out everything that brings misery, poverty, superstition and corruption. His mission is to create happiness for his people, to give them the whole world and he will achieve this by any means, even by a massacre: "They deserved nothing less than the truth—a vacant universe and a cooling world, the right to be happy in anyway they chose. He was quite prepared to make a massacre for their sakes . . . He wanted to begin the world again with them, in a desert."[67] To the Lieutenant, there is nothing unique or mysterious about human existence and human beings have only material needs. His ideal is the well-fed and well-clad but soul-less person. But at the novel's close when he has arrested the Whisky-Priest, he seems to be shaken by the faith of the Priest and feels lost as if life has drained out of the world. The loss of emotion carries him beyond rationalism into a mystical state when he fails to understand why the Priest—of all the people—"should have stayed when the others ran".[68]

The dynamic love which used to move his trigger-finger is dead now though he is sure "it will come back".[69] However, he has begun to sympathize with and admire the Priest: "You are not a bad fellow. If there's anything I can do for you."[70] It is against the law he is supposed to preserve, he runs to fetch Padre Jose to hear the Priest's confession and also arranges whisky for him. The Whisky-Priest represents the force of the irrational whose superiority the novel seeks to establish.

The imagery and the characters of the novel offer a telling picture of the hopeless mess the contemporary life is in. Stripped of family, home and country, man today is drifting from place to place in search of livelihood. A victim to the complexity of modern life, he has lost the capacity to discriminate between the merely superfluous and the really indispensable. Man's preoccupation with money has become so extremely dictatorial that it prevents him from thinking about the higher goals of living and attending to the higher business of finding his soul.

The novel is set in a fever-stricken Mexican State, a land of heat, vulture and swamp: "...the swamp and vultures and no children anywhere, except a few in the village with bellies swollen by worms who ate dirt from the bank, inhumanly." "Heat", "vultures", "decaying teeth" are symbols. "Heat" signifies restlessness and anxiety that man feels today, "vultures" are the symbols of human monstrosity and greed and "decaying teeth" stand for the stinking decay of civilization. Mr. Tench, a morose expatriate English dentist, is a typical Greene figure of decay. Without a memory and without a hope, he is making a bare living out of the decay he cannot prevent. Cut off from his wife and children, he pursues the ugly profession of a dentist in the unhealthy climate and the hopeless conditions of life, the sweat and mosquitoes making life unbearably painful. His greed for money has petrified his heart and the heat and shoddiness have drained away all initiatives. That is the whole world to Mr. Tench: "the heat and the forgetting, the putting off till tomorrow."[72] Mr. Tench is gripped with an awful sense of nausea and longs to escape, but there is no escape for him. He envies the priest: "You are lucky. You can get out. You haven't got your capital here."[73] His possessions—"the Japanese drill, the dentist's chair, the spirit lamp and the pliers and the little oven for the gold fillings: a stake in the country"[74]—define his misery and exile as Minty's possessions emphasize his desperate attempt to feel at home in a foreign land.

Captain Fellows, the English planter, is another rootless man living in exile for a job. Cut off from the whole world, he and his wife long to keep themselves aloof from the local politics because they think that they are foreigners and have "no business interfering with politics".[75] Suffering from headache in the foreign land unsuited for health, Mrs. Fellows complains—"A cookan heat. You know it will kill me to stay"[76] and insists on going back to their place, but Captain Fellows cannot leave because "A man here can do a job of work."[77] The Fellows face the vacuum created by the death of their daughter, Coral, a precocious girl, receiving the right kind of education from her mother, living in the adult world in full ignorance of the word "play" and looking after all the household affairs. She is the product of a topsy-turvy state of affairs in which the distinction between childhood and adulthood is blurred and a child is made to face the responsibilities of adult life much earlier than he is prepared for it. The result is disastrous. Hardy's Father Time kills his brothers and sisters and then commits suicide. Greene's Coral Fellows, without the ghastly morbidity of Father Time, meets a similar end. She quietly and mysteriously vanishes from the scene. Whether she also commits suicide as a result of "pregnancy"[78]—or some other cause, is an open question. But she illustrates the disastrous effects of the modern mechanical civilization on the innocence of childhood.

Padre Jose, the old, fat and ugly priest, is another inhabitant of this shabby land. Giving up his faith, he has married in obedience to the law that all priests should marry. He has no sense of self-respect and, though mocked and taunted both in his home and outside, his only concern is to earn a livelihood. As the habit of self-analysis enables him to see himself as he is—"fat and ugly and old and humiliated"[79]—he is in the grip of the unforgivable sin, despair. Unwilling to get out of this state of despair, he asks the Priest, "Go . . . go. I don't want martyrs here. I don't belong any more. Leave me alone. I'm all right as I am."[80] Lost in the trivialities of life, Padre Jose tries to be another self.

The Half-Caste, "with two fang-like teeth jutting out over his lip,"[81] exemplifies serpentine slipperiness and treachery. Pretending to be an honest Christian eager to help the Priest, he is alway planning to trap him. Eventually, he does succeed and he gets the reward. However, he does not seem to feel any compunction or repentance. He reminds us of Gentleman Brown of Conrad's *Lord*

Jim. As Gentleman Brown is reducing Jim to his own level, the Half-Caste has a grievance against the Priest till the end and tries to reduce him to his own level: "There's not much charity in you, Father. You thought all along I was going to betray you."[82]

These characters truly represent the modern man, engrossed with the material, forgetting the world of the spirit. Superficiality and loss of contact with the world of human emotions characterize man's life in our time. Against a background of these men representing various forms of loneliness and isolation, Greene sets the story of the hunted Priest, his pursuit and capture.

Like Pinkie, the Whisky-Priest is an angst-ridden character. His anxiety arises from an awareness of isolation and from the feeling that he has fallen far short of the glory of God. He fears that he can do nothing to redeem himself. He is the last priest, because the others have either fled or conformed themselves to the law or they have been persecuted and hunted down by the police. In his present condition an outcast and a sinner, the Priest is a parody of a true, official priest as the abandoned wounded bitch gnawing a piece of bone in the deserted banana station of Captain Fellows is "the parody of a watch dog".[83] Exhausted and abandoned, he guards, like the bitch, his last possession, *i.e.*, faith. But the bitch retains hope; it knows no despair. The Priest, on the other hand, is troubled by a sense of sharp contrast between what he was before and his present state. Now shaken by the sense of his own worthlessness, the Priest prays to God to send a more worthy man to carry on the mission he has taken upon himself: "Oh God, send them someone more worthwhile to suffer for. It seemed to him a damnable mockery that they should sacrifice themselves for a whisky-priest with a bastard child."[84]

The Whisky-Priest's past and present point to the modes of existence elaborated by Kierkegaard. As his remorseful conscience reveals, in his early life the Whisky-Priest was living on the aesthetic level of existence. He was just a vain formalistic priest, his hypocrisy, selfishness, pride and lack of love shut out from him the understanding of both God and man. He was just "a play-actor".[85] In the savage scrutiny of his own being "he was proud, lustiful, envious, cowardly and ungrateful."[86] He himself ate good meals in comfortable quarters and slaked his own thirst rather than that of the lost souls. He never experienced the sense of companionship with the pious people who "came kissing his black cotton glove".[87]

Being the last priest, he takes upon himself, at the risk of his life, the task of carrying God to the people. His "courage to be" enables him to affirm his humanity amidst terrible uncertainty of the world. Through a sudden leap he reaches the ethical plane of existence. During the perilous journey he performs through the mountains and forests, he encounters people who signify some important aspects of the human condition and gains a better understanding of himself and life. In the state of corruption he learns to love the poor and the unhappy and identifies himself with the common men—sinners and criminals. In the wretched prison cell he has a feeling of communion with his fellow prisoners. Touched by an extraordinary affection, he feels that he is just "one criminal among a herd of criminals . . ."[88] and becomes aware that the world is like a prison: "overcrowded with lust and crime and unhappy love".[89] Through adultery he finds in himself the capacity for love. Worried about the safety of Brigitta, the fruit of his sin, the Priest strikes a bargain with God and enters into an "I-Thou" relationship with God: "Oh God, give me any kind of death—without contrition, in a state of sin—only save this child."[90] The Priest's prayer anticipates Scobie's in *The Heart of the Matter* and Sarah's in *The End of the Affair*. Before death, the Priest liberates himself from the haunting fear of death and despair and realizes the true meaning of love or of the motto equating God with love. Safe across the border in the neighbouring State, the Priest is moved by a sense of duty and walks back into the trap laid for him. He lays down his life for God and His beloved and accomplishes the greatest act of love. According to the orthodox doctrine the Priest dies in a state of mortal sin, but he does not fear damnation. Even the fear of pain remains in the background. He feels only an immense disappointment that he is going to God "empty-handed, with nothing done at all".[91] This is the sign of humility and modesty which characterize Kierkegaard's spiritual man. In this way the Priest moves away from the rigidity of an official, authoritative and egotistical priest to the gradual attainment of the nature and function of a genuine one. He realizes that the meaning of God and the purpose of life rest ultimately in the mission of love. He proceeds towards the supreme level of existence in fear, pain and loathing and embraces his ultimate victory in death.

The novel hints at Greene's dissatisfaction with the forms of organized religion. Formalistic religion suspends one's imagination, its piety is soulless. In her lack of love and sympathy, the pious, unimaginative woman, who is outraged by the screams of pleasure coming from a man and a woman copulating at the far end of the dark cell, exemplifies the death of the spirit. Her figure deepens this meaning more substantially when the Priest finds her sleeping with "her prim mouth open, showing strong teeth like tombs".[92] His own past is mirrored back to him—a similar figure, not an agent of God but of death.

Thus Greene, in the present novel, emphasizes the theme of man's alienation and protests against the totalitarian Government interfering with human activities and insisting on conformity. He denounces the State which does not think in terms of human beings and tends to persecute an enemy for the common good. He is also opposed to the church as an organized institution because it limits the individual's freedom. The Whisky-Priest attains self-hood by his own effort and quest and gains strength by experience and not by argument or dogma. He lays stress on the gulf lying between the rational and the irrational. The Lieutenant, believing in social utopia and the secular logic of human development, pleads for the satisfaction of material needs and fails to understand how pain and suffering may be good. The Priest, on the other hand, believes in the inevitability of pain and suffering and insists on spiritual satisfaction. Both of them develop a reluctant liking for each other. As the Lieutenant admires the Priest, the Priest admires the Lieutenant: "You're a good man. You've got nothing to be afraid of."[93] Greene appears to be pleading for a proper harmony between the two—the rational and the vital. Thus *The Power and the Glory*, like *Brighton Rock*, underlines the themes of alienation, the significance of human love and suffering and the insignificance of the doctrines and ceremonies of the church.

The Heart of the Matter is concerned with the same existential issues as have been treated in *Brighton Rock* and *The Power and the Glory*. Greene sets the novel in a West African coastal town which, like Brighton and Mexico, is a picture of hell, a province of "Greeneland". The details of the British Colony are based on Greene's actual experience during his stay in Sierra Leone during the years 1941 and 1943. The filthy weather and extremely hot climate are suited for the growth of the ugly fauna—rats, cockroaches, flies and mosquitoes harbouring pestilential diseases and converting the earth into a hell. The imagery derived from the descriptions of natural objects evokes the usual milieu of treachery, violence and lust. The lizard on the wall hunting "for moths and cockroaches",[94] the ugly vulture "flopping from perch to perch",[95] "the rat upon the bath",[96] "the rusty handcuffs",[97] "the broken rosary"[98]—all convey a picture of ugliness and decay. As *The Power and the Glory* is punctuated by the sound of vultures flapping their wings on corrugated iron-roofs, *The Heart of the Matter* is full of references to the continual sights of rats and cockroaches. Greene's carrion birds and beasts are normally conventional symbols of the corruption and horror of a world without God. The natives, Syrians as well as Europeans, are all swallowed up in corruption. "The odour of human meanness and injustice"[99] pervades the entire land. People realize their selfish ends by having recourse to lies, evasions and bribes. Syrians run all the stores in the country and indulge in diamond-smuggling which the Government has failed to control. Yusef, a shameless villain, is a typical representative of this world. He is a smuggler who "sells bad liquor, hoards cottons against a French invasion, seduces the nursing sisters from the military hospital".[100] Wilson and Harris, who are the typical exiles and who are engaged in intrigues, rumours and scandals, are an isolated community. Greene graphically describes their snobbery, meanness and malice. Wilson, the M15 agent, rash, awkward, immature and anxious to adjust himself to the ways of the world, covets Scobie's wife and integrity and spies upon him. A romantic having a great love for poetry, Wilson feels "almost intolerably lonely".[101] Harris, the cable censor, is another version of Minty of *England Made Me*. Living all alone, a pathetic school boy, Harris passes his time in bitter boredom, reading his school magazine and hunting cockroaches. He feels awfully disgusted with the place and the "niggers",[102] who inhabit here. These men are so lost in the material pursuits that they are incapable of any dignified act. Scobie, a just, honest and incorruptible police officer, though the promotion to commissionership, which is his due, is denied to him, chooses to live in this cheap, vulgar place fit for "meanness, malice, snobbery".[103] Even if he is given a job, he won't leave this place, as "he would be lost anywhere else".[104] Scobie's decision to live in a place whose moral and natural conditiions are unfit for decent living, is a sign of protest against the evils of a corrupt urban society, seedy and meretricious. Scobie's love for simple African life is reflected in the folllowing lines:

"Nobody here could ever talk about a heaven on earth. Heaven remained rigidly in its proper place on the other side of death, and on this side flourished the injustices, the cruelties, the meanness that elsewhere people so cleverly hushed up. Here you could love human beings nearly as God loved them, knowing the worst. You didn't love a pose, a pretty dress, a sentiment artfully assumed."[105] Scobie seems to be speaking for Greene himself who felt terribly disgusted with the present ordered and systematized life that breeds brutality, violence and selfishness and who had a great love for the simple, innocent and fresh African life untouched by modern industrialization.

The people, both business men and service-holders with whom Scobie is working, are drawn into the world and have lost their subjectivity or are continuously losing it. They are so lost either in the enhancement of their property or in earning a living that they are unable to experience their dehumanization as despair. Yusef and Tallit are awfully busy in increasing their wealth by all possible means, fair or foul. Similarly, Wilson and Harris accept isolation for their jobs. Lost in the superficiality of life, all of them try to be other than their real selves. Scobie, on the other hand, is conscious of despair, sickness unto death. Like the Whisky-Priest, Scobie is angst-ridden and strives hard to be his real self. His anxiety springs from the conflict of loyalties which torments his mind as well as from an awareness of the absurd in life. Scobie is clear-sighted about the nature of life in the world and knows well from experience that "no human being can really understand another, and no one can arrange another's happiness."[106] He is conscious that it is absurd "to expect happiness in a world so full of misery".[107] Scobie offers an interesting parallel to Conrad's Jim who thinks that man is "incomprehensible",[108] and one never knows what a man is made of. The unbearable sight of misery in the jungle hospital, especially that of the dying child who has survived forty days and nights in the open boat—"the mystery to reconcile that with God"[109] —shakes Scobie and reminds him of his own daughter who died when he was away in Africa. His pity reaches universal proportions and, like the Whisky-Priest, he comes to believe in the inevitability of suffering in the world. He realizes that suffering is inescapable and "To be a human being" one "must drink the cup".[110] Here we are reminded of Dostoyevsky to whom "suffering is life".[111]

Scobie suffers in and for his own life. But he suffers too that which is most illogical and incomprehensible: he suffers in and for the lives of others. Accepting the dialectic, the paradox, the absurdity of existence, Scobie chooses to carry the burden of others' sufferings instead of withdrawing from the world like the heroes of Samuel Beckett. In Beckett the absurd is the spring-board for a leap into actionless subjectivity. Beckett's heroes move from the world of action into the world of contemplation. But Scobie is a typical Greene hero who takes steps to satisfy his needs, and all he needs is "happiness for others and solitude and peace for himself".[112] Scobie, however, has no chance for peace and happiness in this miserable world: they are always dreams of solitude, of quiet changeless cool darkness—"being in darkness, alone with the rain falling, without love or pity".[113] Similarly, his efforts to arrange happiness for others result in suffering for him as well as for others. The emotion of pity leads him to deviate from his own standard of conduct. His professional integrity is shaken, first, when he feels pity for the Portuguese Captain. He experiences profound emotions of guilt and anguish at finding himself in the rank of corrupt officers. Money corrupts others whereas Scobie is "corrupted by sentiment".[114] The money he borrows for the passage of his wife puts him under an obligation undesirable for a Government servant. His affair with Helen involves him not only with a human being but also with God. His desire for peace and his sense of sharing others' sorrows lead him to despair, "the price one pays for setting oneself an impossible aim."[115] Despair is the unforgivable sin but it is a sin a corrupt or evil man never practises. Here one is reminded of Dostoyevsky who thinks that "the decent people who have some conscience and a sense of honour left are in a worse plight."[116] The suffering of the survivors of the shipwreck reduplicates Scobie's despair and offers him "the hint of an explanation—too faint to be grasped",[117] which prompts him to enter into an "I-Thou" relationship with God having an exterior and public expression in the form of a vow or contract. Like the Priest of *The Power and the Glory*, Scobie, unable to bear the heavy uneven breathing of the child, prays to God, "Father, look after her . . give her peace. Take away my peace for ever."[118] Scobie's prayer is addressed to God, who is a "pure thou".[119] Scobie's prayer is an offering of a man who stands naked before God with nothing in his hands. There is no sham or tie. The godhead becomes for him a personal image of father, helper, law-giver and judge. God is near in the image of a person. In a letter to the French Christian existentialist Marcel, Greene puts Scobie's case plainly enough: "Obviously one did have in mind that when he offered up his peace for the child, it was a genuine prayer and had the result that followed. I always believe that such prayers, though obviously a God would not follow them to the limit of robbing him of a peace for ever, are answered up to the point as a kind of test of a man's sincerity and to see whether in fact the offer was merely based on emotion."[120]

Scobie's prayer is answered: the child has the peace of death and a release from suffering and Scobie's peace is taken away for the rest of his earthly career. This is the major turning point in Scobie's life when pity deepens into horror. He is shaken by a deep sense of horror by Louise's sudden return from South Africa and her insistence on taking communion, his being trapped into smuggling a package of diamonds, and being a half-conscious agent of his own native boy's "murder".[121] He is terribly shocked: "One can strike God once too often. After that does one care what happens?"[122] Now Scobie encounters God, the real living God whose voice is heard from his own conscience. God is no longer an abstract or an ideal for contemplation, but a "Thou" to be faced. His affliction goes so deep that he believes that he has no other choice except self-slaughter to resolve the crisis. A voice within, the voice of God, pleads with him urging him to go on living: "I am not Thou but simply you when you speak to me . . . All you have to do now is ring a bell, go into a box, confess . . . Or if you must, continue rejecting me but without lies any more . . . If you live you will come back to me sooner or later."[123] But the sense of suffering for others dominates all thoughts of confession and repentance. Even the fear of eternal damnation and the total loss of the love of God is not able to deflect him from bearing the burden of others.

Scobie's conduct emphasizes the ethical way of existing. The deep sense of humanity and responsibility motivates Scobie's every deed. Even his suicide is provoked not by a sense of ennui or disgust but by an agonized sense of life. His relations to Louise and Helen are marks of his humanity. Louise, who is no longer young or beautiful, is silly, stupid, whining and unhelpful. Any man less humane than Scobie would thrash her. But he feels bound to her "by the pathos of her unattractiveness"[124] as ugliness bound Arthur Rowe to Anna in *The Ministry of Fear* "more than any beauty could have done".[125] More than thirty years older than Helen, and his body having lost the feeling of lust in the tropical climate, Scobie is still drawn to her by her loneliness and innocence. The child-like ugliness of Helen is "like hand-cuffs on his wrists."[126] He feels no responsibility for the beautiful and the intelligent as "they could find their way".[127] A Catholic convert like Greene himself, Scobie is full of revolt against God who allows senseless suffering of the innocent in the here and now. He can believe in no God who is not "human enough to love"[128] what He has created. The way he carefully plans his suicide and makes it appear a natural death so that his wife and mistress may not suffer, also confirms his love for man. He argues that by killing himself he will stop inflicting pain on those he loves –Louise, Helen and God: "I can't desert either of them while I'm alive, but I can die and remove myself from their blood stream. They are ill with me and I can cure them. And you too God—you are ill with me. You'll be better off if you lose me once and for all."[129] As he swallows the overdose of Evipan tablets he tries to say an act of contrition but he does not "remember what it was that he had to be sorry for".[130] His fatal sense of responsibility stays with him till the end and he reminds us of Arthur Rowe of *The Ministry of Fear* to whom it is "right to risk damnation"[131] for the sake of the people one loves. There is something Christ-like in Scobie's self-sacrifice: "Christ had not been murdered: you could not murder God: Christ had killed himself."[132]

Scobie's conduct appears to fulfil the Pauline doctrine of the extreme form of human love, a willingness to save others through one's own damnation: "If man says I love God, and hateth his brother, he is a liar, for he that loveth not his brother, whom he hath seen, how can he love God whom he hath not seen."[133] The significance of human love is stressed by existential thinkers too. Marcel says: "God does not at all want to be loved by us over against the created. . . The God standing against the created and in some way jealous of his own works is in my eyes nothing but an idol."[134] Scobie's longing for peace through human love calls to mind Dr. Rieux of *The Plague*, who joins the victims of the pestilence "so as to reduce the damage done . . . to discover how one attains to the third category: in other words, to peace."[135]

Greene's reaction against the ossified churchianity is insisted upon in this novel too. Like Christian existentialists, Greene is angry at seeing Christianity reduced to a conventional institution because it takes away all true decisions and all the anxiety and the seriousness involved in the leap of faith. Though a Roman Catholic, Scobie feels sick of his religion which seems to mean nothing to him. He tries to love God but feels "Empty".[136] Father Rank reminds us of Father Talbot whom Greene mentions in his *A Sort of Life*.[137] Like Father Talbot, Father Rank fails to understand Scobie's real problem and utters the Latin words of Absolution which bring no sense of relief to Scobie and which are to him just "a formula . . . a hocus pocus".[138] Scobie's suicide, the unforgivable sin to a Catholic, is a sign of protest against dogma. The novel insists on human suffering producing an "I-thou" encounter with God.

Scobie is torn by a conflict of loyalties—loyalty to his profession, loyalty to his religion and loyalty to his innate humanism. He betrays his Government and violates the rules of his church "with his eyes open and knowing the consequences".[139] The shedding off his loyalties to the norms supplied by the external forces and acting in sincerity to his own self point to Greene's protest against conventional standards of morality, social as well as religious. What matters to Greene is pure human love rather than traditional God or religion. He writes out of human sympathy and understanding and his writing is haunted by the paradox of the innocence of the criminal and the guilt of the faultless. Greene admits in an interview that one of the things which interest him most is "discovering humanity in the apparently inhuman character".[140] Thus *The Heart of the Matter*, like its predecessors, brings out the themes of man's feeling of anxiety for modern life, sickening despair, the significance of faith emerging from human love and suffering, insignificance of institutional Christianity, and it places Greene in the company of Kierkegaard, Marcel, Buber and Tillich.

The End of the Affair, like Greene's other religious novels, is mainly concerned with his leaning towards the force of the irrational, man's sickening despair effecting the leap of faith and his impatience with the church and its dogma. Like Kierkegaard, Greene points out that an existential experience of love and suffering leads the individual to abandon the lower level of existence and rise to the higher one through a leap.

The miracles described in the novel—Sarah's prayer restoring Bendrix's life, "Baptized at two years old, and then beginning to go back to what you can't even remember,"[141] "Rationalist speaker converted by Miraculous Cure,"[142] Parkis's boy being cured by a book of Sarah, Mrs. Miles coming and taking "away the pain—

touching him on the right side of the stomach"[143] confirm the presence of the irrational in life. As these miracles stand out of the grasp of intellect, the rationalists discard them as coincidence. Bendrix, who is determined not to lose his faith in miracles, and who explains them away as coincidences like "two cars with the same figures side by side in a traffic block",[144] represents modern emphasis on too narrow rationalism which is not prepared to accept anything mysterious and inexplicable in life. Greene protests against the despiritualization of modern life which is best understood in terms of the gradual evaporation of our period of authentic "paradigmatic experience".[145] Henry, an important assistant secretary in the Ministry of Pensions, is the typical product of present abstract and calculated systems. As he has come under the possession of complex social machinery, he is completely shut off from himself. His preoccupation with office work has deprived him of his humanity and he has since long ceased to feel any physical desire for Sarah and needs her simply for companionship. Worried and full of despair, Henry is living in terrible insecurity because he feels "excluded from Sarah's confidence",[146] and is afraid of being condemned to a life of terrible loneliness and barren solitude.

Greene reminds us of Kierkegaard's teaching about the stages of life. His chief characters are shown passing from the lower level to the highest level of existence. Both Sarah and Bendrix are in the beginning aesthetes living for the pleasures of the moment. Sarah, a woman of loose moral whose husband is sexually impotent, has adulterous relationship with different kinds of men and Bendrix is only one of many men—the favourite lover for the moment. A woman without scruples, Sarah passionately offers herself to Bendrix, she loves him and believes in him as fervently and deeply as she later believes in God. Impervious to the passage of time, she is concerned with the pleasurable present and commits adultery in her husband's house, remorselessly and "unhaunted by guilt".[147] As she does not believe in God remorse dies with the act. She rises to the ethical plane when she promises to give up her love for the life of Bendrix, knocked out only for a few minutes during the air raid. Like Sarah, Bendrix too, a middle-aged novelist, sensual, sophisticated and agnostic, is living the aesthetic way of life and to him, only the moment matters. A professional writer "praised for his technical ability",[148] he is very methodical and does his quota of work—"daily five hundred words".[149] Nothing, not even a love affair, can upset his self-imposed discipline and alter his schedule. He is not "interested in anything else in the world"[150] except for his writing and feels extremely happy when he conveys his sense and his characters begin to live. While writing his story about the civil servant and trying to understand the working of Sarah's mind, he falls in love with her. This is like a sudden leap which leads Bendrix towards the next higher stage. Bendrix's relation with Sarah, a woman having human weaknesses, is not determined by lust though he is aware of the possibility of falling in love "over a dish of onions".[151] The passion that begins their love affair is afterwards replaced by pure human love. Bendrix, a self-conscious individual, loves Sarah "as a person in her own right—not a part of a house like a bit of porcelain, to be handled with care".[152] It is not simply the "onions" but the "sudden sense of an individual woman, of a frankness"[153] that makes him happy and miserable in later life. Now Bendrix is "human enough to think of another person's trouble",[154] and his relations with Sarah are a part of his humanity.

At the ethical level, both Sarah and Bendrix suffer from a terrible feeling of anxiety and despair, *i.e.*, sickness unto death in Kierkegaard.. Sarah's prayer, "Let him be alive, and I will believe . . . I will give him up for ever, only let him be alive"[155] is along the lines of the prayers of the Whisky-Priest of *The Power and the Glory* and Scobie of *The Heart of the Matter* and fulfils the definition of a genuine prayer given by Gabriel Marcel in his *Metaphysical Journal*: "If you pray with sufficient intensity you will believe that your prayer, if not granted, is at least heard."[156] Uttered in a feeling of contrition, weakness, dependence and humility not in a feeling of consciousness of strength and wisdom, self-reliance and self-importance, a prayer is effective. Sarah, like the Priest and Scobie, prays in a state of powerlessness and hence her prayer is answered. She herself reflects: "When you are helpless enough . . . You can pray for miracles. They happen, don't they, to the poor, and I was poor."[157] Now Sarah, a modern sophisticated woman, very worldly in her sensibility, is tormented by a conflict between her desire to be her own real self and her desire to be another self. Sarah, who is concerned with living in the present without the thought of the past and the future, and whose love for Bendrix continues as strongly as ever, has to reconcile herself to a life without Bendrix. On the other hand, her problem is to discover the identity of Him to Whom the pledge has been made together with the identity of the One Who made her take the vow and prepare herself for the "desert" where "there's nobody nothing, for miles and miles around."[158] Gripped with the absurd dread of the unknown and the feeling of loneliness, emptiness and desolation, Sarah longs to believe "in some kind of a God . . . something vague, amorphous, cosmic . . . stretching out of the vague into the concrete human life, like a powerful vapour,"[159] and to become part of that vapour and escape the seriousness and uncertainty of choice. But she "can't invent a belief".[160] The feelings of misery and emptiness make her rebellious and desperate and like Scobie, she questions the existence of a merciful God: "He doesn't exist . . . He can't exist. You can't have a merciful God and this despair."[161]

Failing to invent belief in God, Sarah tries out other methods to escape self-hood, but there's no escape. She tries to convince herself that a vow to someone she does not believe in is "not all that important"[162] and has recourse to sex and drink to avoid the implication of her vow. "But it doesn't work. It doesn't work any longer."[163] There is no joy left in her life, there is no lust for her either, she can't escape feeling despair. The fanaticism of the rationalist preacher, Richard Smythe with livid spots on his left cheek, whom she visits, hoping that he will convince her to break her bargain, "gives her a sense of inverted belief"[164] and fixes "the superstition deeper".[165] Sarah's desire to believe in absolutes and abstrations and love Bendrix without seeing him proves to be a desperate cry. She cannot believe in anything but her own experience: "Even a God can't love something that doesn't exist, he can't love something he can't see."[166] Thus Sarah's efforts to dispel despair result in its reduplication. Like Sarah, Bendrix too suffers from a deep sense of despair resulting from the frustration of his desire. Shocked by the sudden end of his love affair with Sarah and the vision of her abandoning herself to another man, Bendrix, like Scobie, plans his suicide saving his sleeping pills and is prevented by "the memory of the look of disappointment of Sarah's face".[167] He is filled with revolt against God when his hope to win Sarah from his intangible divine adversary "imprisoned behind the altar"[168] is frustrated and he is condemned to a crippled existence, "the empty life, odourless, antiseptic, the life of a prison".[169] Bendrix's hatred for God is the reflection of his own tormented mind like Lear cursing the elements. In spite of his combat with his rival and firm determination not to surrender himself to Him, he is afraid that his hatred may turn into belief which will be a triumph for God. Bendrix thinks: "Hatred seems to operate the same glands as love, it even produces the same actions."[170]

This comes very close to Dr. Colin's statement in *A Burnt-out Case*: "Love is planted in man now, even uselessly in some cases, like an appendix. Sometimes of course people call it hate".[171] Bendrix is full of hatred for God who remains the tempter and destroyer of human happiness till the end: "You're a devil God, tempting us to leap. . . With Your great schemes You ruin our happiness like a harvester ruins a mouse's nest. I hate You God, I hate You as though You existed."[172] Out of despair, he tries to be another self seducing a younger and more beautiful girl than Sarah on the day of her funeral just to show to dead Sarah that he can do without her. He is dismayed to find that his lust like Sarah's has been corroded as his passion for Sarah has "killed simple lust for ever".[173] A gnawing doubt threatens his profession and agnostic way of life and he feels the insignificance of his art: "If Sarah is right how unimportant all the importance of art is".[174] Bendrix's feeling of anxiety leads him to believe in the existence of God, though he resists the "leap" as it involves a denial of his autonomous existence and all interests in the here and now: ". . . loving him there'd be no pleasure in anything at all with him away. I'd even lose my work, I'd cease to be Bendrix. Sarah, I'm afraid."[175] Bendrix's anxiety about his situation implies anxiety about human situation. Like a natural man, he experiences the absurd in life and sees God as a corruptor of human happiness.

Sarah and Bendrix fulfil the definitions of faith given by the Christian existentialists. They get over doubts, temptations, fears, misery and make movement of faith in fear and trembling. They abandon the lower level of existence and rise to the higher one through a leap, though Bendrix informs ironically he "won't leap".[176] His word "leap" is actually French word *saute* used by the French existentialists to describe the means of rising from one plane of existence to another, the higher one. Sarah, like Kierkegaard's Abraham, walks the narrow path of faith and gradually and painfully realizes God's love. She opens herself to God in a spirit of self-surrender and experiences the delight in spite of all her agony and realizes that her affair with Bendrix was but a figure in the tapestry of divine purpose: "Did I ever love Maurice as much before I loved You? Or was it really You I loved all the time? . . . But You are too good to me. When I ask You for pain You give me peace."[177] Now Sarah has "caught belief like a disease".[178] But her leap is different from what Camus calls "the philosophical suicide" or "the intentional mutilation of the soul".[179] Like the Whisky-Priest and Scobie, Sarah is always seized with a deep sense of human affliction. Her love for Bendrix signifies pure selfless love a human being feels for another. Her love for Bendrix is turned towards *agape* and she responds to the offer of *agape* through an act of charity. She triumphs over her human weaknesses which makes her, like the Whisky-Priest, conscious of her own unworthiness: "I'm a bitch and a fake and I hate myself."[180] Her liking for Richard Smythe, her kindness to the sick boy of Parkis and her willingness to share the misery of Henry with his astigmatism are signs of her deep human love. Sarah, like Mitya of Dostoyevsky, longs to suffer and be cleansed by suffering. She wants to sacrifice herself for the suffering of humanity like christ: "Let me think of those awful spots on Richard's cheek. Let me see Henry's face with tears falling. . . I don't mind my pain. It's their pain I can't stand. . . If I could suffer like you, I could heal like you."[181] Unable to outlive the tension created in her by the conflict between her faith and her overwhelming "ordinary corrupt human love"[182] and touched by universal suffering, she prays to God for death: "I don't know how I am going to live in this pain and longing and I'm praying to God all the time that he won't be hard on me, that he won't keep me alive."[183] Though she does not kill herself like Scobie, her dying of uncared pneumonia, comes very close to self-slaughter.

Bendrix's prayer at the close of the novel to leave him "alone for ever"[184] in a state of anxiety-ridden impatience is suggestive of irrational leap to faith. The prayer calls to mind Job's in the midst of his suffering: "Are not the days of my life few? Let me alone, that I may find a little comfort. . . ."[185] Bendrix recognizes divinity revealed through his own life and Sarah's. But left in a state of uncertainty, he is unclear whether to love or to hate God: "I said to her, I'm a man of hate. But I didn't feel much hatred, I had called other people hysterical, but my own words were overcharged. I could detect their insincerity."[186]

Sarah's feeling of revolt against the priests, who can't understand her situation and sympathize with her, reflects Greene's own impatience with the priests and the rituals of the church. Sarah comments out of disgust: "...to hell with the whole lot of them. . . They are between us and God. . . God has more mercy."[187]

Thus the novel reveals Greene's concern with the themes of Christian existentialism—man's alienation and feeling of despair, human love and suffering inspiring faith and the denunciation of dogma. Greene points out the inadequacy of the rules and the use of religious arguments for faith. Religious experience flowers out of an inner being beyond the reach of rationality and is not to be plucked simply by talking thought. Faith involves a leap beyond reason. Self-knowledge that is a passionate kind of knowledge is more relevant to faith than the reason of the mathematical sort. The leap of faith, however, is not arbitrary. The love of God results from the experience of love of man.

Like other religious novels, Graham Greene's *A Burnt-out Case* presents the theme of man's alienation in the present century, his feeling of anxiety and the significance of human love and suffering in the individual's life. The novel emphasizes Greene's usual criticism of modern life that has deprived man of his existential humanity and his love for the simple and peaceful life of the African natives that is still capable of revitalizing man.

The novel offers an interesting contrast between contemporary civilized life and the primitive African life. The pressures of society exerted largely through the Press mould the lives of the people in stereotyped ways and produce a world of conformists. In such a world the very possibility of choice and decision is taken away. The decisions have already been taken for us, and all we are expected to do is to conform to them and so reinforce them. As a consequence, the modern man is a slave to public opinion and he submits to having all his thinking response and living done for him by others. He has become too enervated to think, respond and act by his own capacity. As he is circumscribed, a natural and spontaneous behaviour on his part is impossible. He is what Heidegger calls "das man", a man lost in the crowd. Instead of living independently and obeying his own inner self, he lives the crowd life. The pressure of the ordered systematized life has made man selfish, brutal and violent, whereas in the primitive way of life man is still full of concern for his fellow-beings. Greene criticizes the dehumanizing elements of modern life, condemns all political and economic progress and reveals a nostalgic longing for more human and personal conditions of life. Through Querry, a world-famous architect, Greene offers a horrifying picture of a man who is sick of European civilization. Bored of his worldly success, Querry tries to escape to a remote leper colony. Driven by a sense of revulsion, he, like Conrad's Jim, wants to be in a place where nothing will remind him of his past when he "was alive, with a vocation and a capacity to love—if it was love".[188] Querry's flight into the heart of darkness, a leproserie deep in the Congo, is a sign of revolt against modern life. Nauseated by the contemporary disorder, Querry seeks refuge in the so-called dark world. His inward hollowness—"Nothing. I want nothing... I suffer from nothing"[189] —is the symbol of the spiritual hollowness of the contemporary materialistic civilization. He represents the bewildered failure of feeling and imagination of our terrible world. The suffering of the world's untouchables, the humanity of Doctor Colin and the priests, the peaceful life of the leproserie stir a sense of kinship with the people in distress and revive his love for man. The representatives of the civilized world, on the other hand, which Querry has left behind, stand as hurdles in the way of his self-knowledge. Rycker, the manager of a palm oil plantation, a smug, pious, formalistic, self-centred Catholic, is a dehumanized figure. A man interested in moral theology, he bores his young wife with his spiritual discussions. He is proud, full of self-importance and has no genuine sympathy for the lepers. He helps the mission only out of charity. Rycker propagates Querry's presence in the colony and puts in his way Parkinson, a vulgar, corrupt, English journalist, so as to obstruct Querry's self-knowledge. With the arrival of Parkinson, the great world, which Querry has left, makes a path to his door and Querry's quest for identity is interrupted by the sensational and ridiculous accounts of his achievements spread by the journalist. The doppleganger motive suggested in the relationship between the Whisky-Priest and the Half-Caste and between Scobie and Yusef is hinted at here. As Jim finds his own reflection in Gentleman Brown, Querry feels that Parkinson is a looking glass which "returns such a straight image".[190] Writing articles entitled "An Architect of Souls," "The Hermit of Congo", Parkinson destroys Querry's dream of "pendele".[191] Doctor Colin aptly reflects: "The fools, the interfering fools, they exist everywhere, ... He had been cured of all but his success; but you can't cure success.... Success is like that too—a mutilation of the natural man."[192]

The novel lays stress on the ethical way of existence. Doctor

Colin and the priests of the mission are dedicated to the improvement of the hospital and to the welfare of the lepers. The priests are not as much interested in the rules and the conventions of the church as in the service of the patients. They are "unconcerned with private lives"[193] and their tolerance encompasses even atheists and unmarried parishioners who have a baby each year from a different man. As they are interested in the welfare of the people, they are against wasting money on a church because "the people still live in mud huts".[194] The Superior, who is more endearing and charitable than others, is a humanist to whom human love is superior to the divine love. The Superior reflects: "I do not tell you to do good things for the love of God. That is very hard. Too hard for many of us. It is much easier to show mercy because a child weeps or to love because a girl or a young man pleases your eye."[195]

Like the priests, Doctor Colin too is only concerned with the betterment of human condition. James Noxon has aptly remarked: "In a merciless climate, against official parsimony and native suspicion, he works to salvage the diseased wreckage that an indifferent nature throws his way."[196] Unlike the Fathers, he has no belief in God to support him in his hard vocation and one can learn from him that "it's possible for an intelligent man to make his life without a god."[197] Examining a three-year-old leper, the doctor says to the Superior, "Your God must feel a bit disappointed when he looks at this world of his."[198] The Superior's reply—"God cannot feel disappointment nor pain"[199]—is not convincing. The doctor does not need a God who is incapable of pain. He says, "Perhaps that's why I don't care to believe in Him."[200] Here one is reminded of Camus's Dr. Rieux confronting the Bishop of Oran with, "Until my dying day, I shall refuse to love a scheme of things in which children are put to torture."[201] Dr. Rieux is unwilling to cease curing the sick and to leave that to an all-powerful God. Behind their selfless service, the chief motive of Dr. Rieux as well as of Dr. Colin is their deep sense of sharing human suffering. Dr. Rieux says: "There are sick people and they need curing."[202] As Dr. Rieux offers himself to fight out the disease just for the sake of "common decency that consists in doing"[203] his job, Dr. Colin wants to put himself "in touch with the whole human condition"[204] by means of "the search for suffering and the remembrance of suffering".[205]

Living away from the modern busy civilized life, Doctor Colin and the priests are endowed with all the laudable qualities that distinguish man from animals, while Querry, born and brought up in the city, suffers from alienation. No longer an aesthete designing a building or making love to a woman for his own solitary pleasure, infected with the boredom of a satiated man, Querry lapses into cynical detachment from the aesthetic way of life and swings from the mood of enjoyment to the mood of melancholy, *i.e.* despair and sickness unto death. Self-love and self-expression, which were behind all he did, have destroyed everything, even his true self, because "self-expression is a hard and selfish thing. It eats everything, even the self".[206] Querry parallels Karenin of Tolstoy, whose life had been geared to professional ambition and who felt totally isolated in his misery. Querry's heart is burnt out and his spiritual condition resembles the physical state of a leper who, though technically cured, is mutilated. Querry is aware of the loss of his identity, and self-identity is his only concern: "I am looking after myself. . .".[207] He is totally vacant and feels no pity for the miserable life of the lepers. "Human beings are not my country",[208] he writes in his journal. Like Conrad's Jim who feels "responsible for every life in the land,"[209] Querry tries to ease his bleeding conscience by working for the people in a place where he is a stranger. He begins a slow and painful recovery of his real self amid the squalor and suffering at the leproserie. The first sign of the stiring of a new life is seen when his negro boy, Deo Gratias, has an accident and Querry goes out into the bush to rescue him. This accident gives him "an odd feeling"[210] that he is needed. Gradually Querry has a twinge of suffering and begins "to feel part of the human condition".[211] The suffering of the African lepers brings about a remarkable change in Querry's heart and he begins to feel responsible for them. With the resurgence of human feeling he allows himself to be persuaded to design the building of the new hospital and in this way he makes himself useful to the mission. Though his desire to reach "pendele", the place of contentment, does not materialize, he is killed when his shrivelled soul is coming to life again in a kind of resurrection, the spiritual leper is healed before his death. The parable he narrates to Mary Rycker is a sort of confession that gives him a sense of freedom and release from the past. He regains his real self through suffering. He reflects: "I think I am cured of pretty well everything, even disgust. I've been happy here."[212]

Querry reminds us of Greene himself who was awfully bored with life, flirted with fake suicide so as to overcome the feeling of boredom, and discovered a love of life during his Liberian trip. Querry bears a striking resemblance to Beckett's Murphy who escapes from the world which has seemed to him "a colossal fiasco"[213] and enters the asylum for lunatics as a male nurse. As Querry is followed by Rycker and Parkinson, Murphy is hunted by five persons who seek him out of erotic and other interests. Murphy, whose "conarium has shrunk to nothing"[214] and whose mind is "a large hollow sphere, hermetically closed to the universe without"[215] is seeking "the best of himself".[216] The doctors and the visitors stimulate his sense of kinship with the patients and now he can "mix with them, touch them, speak to them, watch them and imagine himself one of them."[217] One may note a few points of comparison between Querry and Jean Tarrou of Camus's *The Plague*. Nauseated with the unjust and meaningless world, Tarrou, like Querry, retreats into a plague-stricken town, Oran. As Querry feels like a leper, Tarrou "has plague already"[218] long before he comes to this town, encounters it here and is anxious to "get out of it".[219] Querry is looking for a reason for living and finds one in being useful to the lepers; Tarrou longs for peace through serving others. He thinks he must do what he can "to cease being plague-stricken and that is the only way in which we can hope for some peace."[220]

Though Querry, like Greene himself, finds an interest in the act of living, he is caught in a struggle between belief and unbelief. The Priest and Scobie are believers, Sarah yields to believe and Bendrix resists belief. But all these stances are merged in Querry who is always troubled by his lack of faith and keeps on "fingering it like a sore"[221] which he wants to get rid of, as Dr. Colin puts it. Querry's soul is always in a state of restlessness because it is constantly looking for itself and does not find itself. This kind of absence of itself from itself is suggestive of the state of being on the way tending towards God. This indicates that Querry has attained faith. The line from Pascal that the Superior quotes is applicable to him: "A man who starts looking for God, has already found him. The same may be true of love—when we look for it, perhaps we've already found it."[222] Thus Querry comes very close to the ideal of Kierkegaard's spiritual man. He gets a moment of insight into himself through suffering—"suffering is the distinguishing quality of religious action"[223] according to Kierkegaard. Querry has shaken off all attachments of the world and has given up his desire to rise to the height of worldly achievements. Querry who has conquered his mind and subdued his sex-instinct and who is free from passion, fear and anger, appears to be coming very close to the ideal of the 'Sthita Prajna" of the *Bhagavad-Gita.* Even the scandal and abuses of Rycker do not disturb his modesty. Not afraid of his own death he feels pity for Mary Rycker who sticks to her lies as "They are her only way of escape from Rycker and Africa".[224] He dies laughing and murmuring, "Absurd, this is absurd or else".[225] This is a right comment on not only his own life in which success and fulfilment have been deceptive but also on life in general. His last words suggest that life and death are meaningless and they acquire meaning in some transcendental pattern offered by religion or in the pattern of Dr. Colin.

Thus the novel conveys Greene's reaction against the present industrialized civilization that has dehumanized man, and his love for the simple, innocent and peaceful primitive life. It points out that theological discussions and the observance of dogmas are not relevant to faith that results from human love and suffering. Laying stress on these themes Greene joins the company of the Christian existentialists.

This brief survey of Greene's important religious novels reveals his close affinity with the Christian existentialists. Like Kierkegaard, Marcel, Jaspers, Buber and Tillich, Greene is ill at ease with the boredom, vulgarity and seediness of the modern civilization in which the springs of life have dried up and man has lost his true self. He is critical of the dehumanizing effects of the present civilization and suggests, through characters like Scobie and Querry, an escape to the primitive African life, which is much superior to our chrome-and-neon civilization. Greene is deeply shocked by the despiritualization of modern life on account of too much emphasis on materialistic outlook. The liberal outlook that believes in social progress is undermined, as it ignores the presence of the irrational and incongruous elements in life. Greene rejects the conventional middle class values that Ida Arnold of *Brighton Rock* and the Lieutenant of Police of *The Power and the Glory* represent and insists on the significance of the authentic experience of the mysterious which has evaporated in our time as a result of scientific progress. Without the experience of this kind, Greene thinks that no consistent conduct and no real human existence are possible. Hostile to the rigid calculating rules of life in which modern scientific rationalism is interested, and believing in the endless possibilities of human life and limitless power of human spirit, Greene emphasizes the existential character of man who is someone to whom concrete facts of life are closer than concepts and for whom the real may not be equivalent to the intelligible. Faith is still present and wages a ceaseless war against the rational outlook, as is seen in *The Power and the Glory* and *The End of the Affair*. A champion of individual freedom, Greene denounces the church and its rigid dogmatic rituals because they deprive man of his independent decision, as is seen in the priests of *Brighton Rock* and *The Heart of the Matter*. To Greene, as to the Christian existentialists, faith which is an inward experience and which flows from man's internal resources beyond the grasp of human intelligence is important. All his heroes—Rose, Priest, Scobie, Sarah, Bendrix and Querry—reach spirituality without following the rules of the church, they possess, what Professor Tillich calls, "the courage of despair" and affirm their humanity in the terrible moments of their life. Though through a "leap of faith" they encounter the living God in an "I-thou" relationship, their faith is not unconditional nor arbitrary: it is, rather, like the faith of Kierkegaard's Abraham who did not believe that some day he would be blessed in the beyond, but that he would be happy here in the world, earth-bound. Rose, Priest, Scobie, Sarah, Bendrix and Querry realize divine love only after suffering human love. Speaking on the interdependence of the divine and the human love, Querry appears to be speaking for Greene himself: "Perhaps it is true that you can't believe in a God without loving a human being or love a human being without believing in a God."[226]

In the introductory essay to his anthology *Existentialism from Dostoyevsky to Sartre*, Walter Kaufmann explains his omission of the religious existentialists on the ground that "religion has always been existentialist"[227] which seems to others more a reason for including them than for excluding them. In a similar fashion, what has been emphasized here as Greene's existential bias, may be regarded by some as religious bias. Religion is not simply a detached observation of rituals for its own sake. Rather it is a way of life. It always stands in need of existential verification in the lived life of men. On the other hand, through the dual need of expressing religious reality and of handing it down, religion produces schools of thoughts and bodies of beliefs which lead in very different directions from man's concrete existence. It is understandable, therefore, that the life of every religion depends not only upon its continuation but upon those men within it who will bring it back to the concrete reality from which it began. As Greene insists on the incessant return to the lived religious life and on the superior reality of the religious meeting with reality over any formulations concerning the nature of religious reality, he may properly be called an existentialist. Greene, like an existentialist, speaks of God, not on the basis of a rational argument, establishing God's existence but as a result of a reflection on the meaning of human existence, when it is explored to its furthest boundaries. Greene's insistence on man's freedom of faith reminds us of Dostoyevsky to whom "material proofs"[228] are irrelevant for faith. Greene joins the contemporary writers in whom "a sense of human affliction"[229] is one of the most revealing gestures of the modern world and the modern man.

Notes and References

1. S. Kierkegaard, *The Point of View for My Work as an Author*, trans. Walter Lowrie (New York, 1939), p. 193.
2. Heidegger, *Being and Time*, trans. J. Macquarrie and E.S. Robinson (New York and London, 1962), p. 163.
3. Karl Jaspers, *Man in the Modern Age*, trans. Eden and Cedar Paul (New York: Doubleday Anchor Books, 1956).
4. C. Marcel, *Homo Viator*, trans. E. Craufurd (New York: Harper and Brothers, 1951).
5. —, *Metaphysical Journal*, pp. 329-30-
6. Martin Buber, *Pointing The Way*, Ed. and trans. Maurice Friedman (New York: Harper Torch-Books, 1963), p. 27.
7. Kierkegaard, *Fear and Trembling and Sickness Unto Death*, trans. Walter Lowrie (New York: Doubleday Anchor Books, 1954), p. 180.
8. G. Marcel, *The Philosophy of Existentialism*, trans. Manya Harari (New York: Philosophical Library, 1956), p. 15.
9. *Homo Viator*, p. 36.
10. *Ibid.*, p. 39.
11. *Man in the Modern Age*, p. 202.
12. *Ibid.*, p. 210.
13. K. Jaspers, *The Origin and Goal of History*, trans. Michael Bullock (New Haven and London, 1953), p. 2.
14. Paul Tillich, *The Courage to Be* (New Haven: Yale University Press, 1952), p. 142.
15. S. Kierkegaard, *The Concluding Unscientific Postscript*, trans. David F. Swenson (Princeton: Princeton University Press, 1941), p. 277.
16. —, *Fear and Trembling*, trans. W. Lowrie (New York: Doubleday, 1954), p. 85.
17. —, *Attack Upon Christendom*, trans. W. Lowrie (London: O.U.P., 1944), p. 221.
18. *The Concluding Unscientific Postscript*, p. 42.
19. W. Shakespeare, *Hamlet*, Act II, ii, Lines 249-50.
20. *The Concluding Unscientifiic Postscript*, p. 178.
21. *Ibid.*, p. 182.

22. *Metaphysical Journal*, p. 237.
23. *Ibid.*, p. 158. 24. *Ibid.*, p. 160.
25. Martin Buber, *I and Thou*, trans. Ronal Gregor Smith (New York: Charles Scribner's Sons, 1958), p. 56.
26. Paul Tillich, *Dynamics of Faith* (New York: Harper Torch Books, 1958), p. 102.
27. Karl Jaspers, *Philosphie Vol. III, Metaphysics*, trans. Marga Frank and Arthur Newton (Berlin: Springer Verlag, 1932), p. 167.
28. Graham Greene, *Brighton Rock* (London: William Heinemann Ltd., 1938), Penguin Books, 1974, p. 37.
29. *Ibid.*, p. 69.
30. *Being and Time*, p. 319.
31. *Brighton Rock*, p. 114.
32. *Ibid.*, p. 129. 33. *Ibid.*, p. 81.
34. "What was most evil in him needed her, it could not get along without goodness." *Ibid.*, p. 127.
35. *Ibid.*, p. 67.
36. "She knew by tests as clear as mathematics that Pinkie was evil." *Ibid.*, p. 201.
37. *Ibid.*, p. 200. 38. *Ibid.*, p. 241.
39. *Ibid.*, p. 93. 40. *Ibid.*, p. 102.
41. *Ibid.*, p. 167. 42. *Ibid.*, p. 241.
43. *Ibid.*, p. 53. 44. *Ibid.*, p. 230.
45. Greene's concept of "hell" comes closer to that of Dostoyevsky. Hell in Dostoyevsky is suffering "that comes from the consciousness that one is no longer able to love." F. Dostoyevsky, *The Brothers Karamazov*, I., trans. David Magarshack (London: Hazell Watson & Viney Ltd., 1958), Penguin Books, 1976, p. 380.
46. *Brighton Rock*, p. 229.
47. *Ibid.*, p. 113. 48. *Ibid.*, p. 229. 49. *Ibid.*, p. 241.
50. *Ibid.*, p. 244. 51. *Ibid.*, p. 249. 52. *Ibid.*, p. 250.
53. *Ibid.*, p. 242. 54. *Ibid.*, p. 230. 55. *Ibid.*, p. 234.
56. *Ibid.*, p. 191. 57. *Ibid.*, p. 196. 58. *Ibid.*, p. 244.
59. *Ibid.*, p. 110. 60. *Ibid.*, p. 242.
61. "It was as if he'd been withdrawn suddenly by a hand out of any existence—past or present, whipped away into zero—nothing." *Ibid.*, p. 245.
62. *Ibid*, p. 248. 63. *Ibid.*, p. 249.

64. "Believe that God loves you in a way you cannot even conceive of. He loves you in spite of your sin and in your sin." *The Brothers Karamazov*, I, p. 56.
65. Graham Greene, *The Power and the Glory* (London: William Heinemann Ltd., 1940), Penguin Books, 1974, p. 24.
66. *Ibid.*, p. 25. 67. *Ibid.*, p. 58. 68. *Ibid.*, p. 195.
69. *Ibid.*, p. 220. 70. *Ibid.* p. 201. 71. *Ibid.*, p. 34.
72. *Ibid.*, p. 8. 73. *Ibid.*, p. 17. 74. *Ibid.*
75. *Ibid.*, p. 37. 76. *Ibid.*, p. 213. 77. *Ibid.*
78. Atkins assumes that "she was pregnant". *Graham Greene*, p. 120.
79. *The Power and the Glory*, p. 49.
80. *Ibid.*, p. 118. 81. *Ibid.*, p. 105. 82. *Ibid.*, p. 197.
83. *Ibid.*, p. 142. 84. *Ibid.*, p. 135. 85. *Ibid.*, p. 162.
86. *Ibid.*, p. 95. 87. *Ibid.*, p. 128. 88. *Ibid.*
89. *Ibid.*, p. 125. 90. *Ibid.*, p. 82. 91. *Ibid.*, p. 210.
92. *Ibid.*, p. 133. 93. *Ibid.*, p. 206.
94. Graham Greene, *The Heart of the Matter* (London: William Heinemann Ltd., 1948), Penguin Books, 1962, p. 55.
95. *Ibid.*, p. 13. 96. *Ibid.*, p. 57. 97. *Ibid.*, p. 72.
98. *Ibid.*, p. 176. 99. *Ibid.*, p. 15. 100. *Ibid.*, p. 67.
101. *Ibid.*, p. 11.
102. "I hate the place, I hate the people. I hate the bloody niggers." *The Heart of the Matter*, p. 13.
103. *Ibid.*, p. 31. 104. *Ibid.*, p. 23. 105. *Ibid.*, p. 35.
106. *Ibid.*, p. 81. 107. *Ibid.*, p. 117.
108. "It is when we try to grapple with another man's intimate need that we perceive how incomprehensible, wavering and misty are the beings that share with us. . . ." *Lord Jim*, p. 138.
109. *The Heart of the Matter*, p. 114. 110. *Ibid.*, p. 118.
111. "Well, of course, they suffer, but they live, they live a real and not an illusory life, for suffering is life." *The Brothers Karamazov*, II, p. 755.
112. *The Heart of the Matter*, p. 181.
113. *Ibid.*, p. 128.
114. *The Heart of the Matter*, p. 53.
115. *Ibid.*, p. 58.
116. *The Brothers Karamazov*, II, p. 757.
117. *The Heart of the Matter*, p. 114.
118. *Ibid.*, p. 118.
119. "To pray is to actively refuse to think God as order, it is to

think him as really God, as pure Thou." *Metaphysical Journal*, p. 160.

120. Quoted in M. Mesnet's *Graham Greene and the Heart of the Matter*, p. 102.

121. "I did not cut his throat myself, but he died because I existed." *The Heart of the Matter*, p. 241.

122. *Ibid.*, p. 235. 123. *Ibid.*, p. 250. 124. *Ibid.*, p. 27.

125. Graham Greene, *The Ministry of Fear* (London: William Heinemann Ltd., 1943), Penguin Books, 1964, p. 207.

126. *The Heart of the Matter*, p. 152.

127. *Ibid.* 128. *Ibid.*, p. 114.

129. *Ibid.*, pp. 249-50. 130. *Ibid.*, p. 256.

131. *The Ministry of Fear*, p. 132.

132. *The Heart of the Matter*, p. 182.

133. "The Book of I John", *The Bible*, ch. 4, p. 20.

134. G. Marcel, *Being and Having: An Existential Diary*, trans. K. Farrer (New York: Harper and Brothers, 1949), p. 42.

135. A. Camus, *The Plague*, trans. Stuart Gilbert (London: Hamish Hamilton, 1948, Penguin Books, 1976, p. 208.

136. "I feel—tired of my religion. It seems to mean nothing to me. I've tried to love God . . . But I feel—empty. Empty." *The Heart of the Matter*, p. 146.

137. *A Sort of Life*, p. 138.

138. *The Heart of the Matter*, p. 146.

139. *Ibid.*, p. 191.

140. *The Hindustan Times, Sunday Magazine*, September 29, 1957, p. 3, col. 3.

141. Graham Greene, *The End of the Affair* (London: William Heinemann Ltd., 1951), Penguin Books, 1975, p. 187.

142. *Ibid.*, p. 189. 143. *Ibid.*, p. 178. 144. *Ibid.*, p. 189.

145. Karl Mannheim, *Diagnosis of Our Time* (New York: O.U.P., 1944), p. 146.

146. *The End of the Affair*, p. 42.

147. *Ibid.*, p. 50, 148. *Ibid.*, p. 7. 149. *Ibid.*, p. 19.

150. *Ibid.*, p. 43.

151. "Onions" is a code word for passion. Love becomes Onions, even the act itself "Onions". *The End of the Affair*, p. 53.

152. *Ibid.*, p. 18. 153. *Ibid.*, p. 44.

154. *Ibid.*, p. 41. 155. *Ibid.*, p. 95.

156. *Metaphysical Journal*, p. 225.

157. *The End of the Affair*, p. 73.
158. *Ibid.*, p. 93. 159. *Ibid.*, p. 109. 160. *Ibid.*, p. 91.
161. *Ibid.*, p. 93. 162. *Ibid.* 163. *Ibid.*, p. 101.
164. *Ibid.*, p. 115. 165. *Ibid.* 166. *Ibid.*, p. 101.
167. *Ibid.*, p. 75. 168. *Ibid.*, p. 128. 169. *Ibid.*, p. 145.
170. *Ibid.*, p. 27.
171. Graham Greene, *A Burnt-out Case* (London: William Heinemann, 1961), Penguin Books, 1973, p. 124.
172. *The End of the Affair*, p. 191.
173 *Ibid.*, p. 58. 174. *Ibid.*, p, 148. 175. *Ibid.*, p. 182.
176. *Ibid.*, p. 190. 177. *Ibid.*, p. 122. 178. *Ibid.*, p. 147.
179. *The Myth of Sisyphus*, p. 41.
180. *The End of the Affair*, p. 95.
181. *Ibid.*, p. 120. 182. *Ibid.*, p. 89. 183. *Ibid.*, p. 146.
184. *Ibid.*, p. 192.
185. "The Book of Job", *The Bible*, Chapter 10, p. 20.
186. *The End of the Affair*, p. 190.
187. *Ibid.*, p. 147.
188. *A Burnt-out Case*, p. 46.
189. *Ibid.*, p. 16. 190. *Ibid.*, p. 116.
191. "Pendele" is the word uttered by Deo Gratias in the darkness of the forest where Querry finds him caught in a shallow marsh and the word stands for a place of "singing and dancing and games and prayers." *Ibid.*, p. 58.
192. *Ibid.*, p. 197. 193. *Ibid.*, p. 120. 194. *Ibid.*, p. 71.
195. *Ibid.*, pp. 81-2.
196. James Noxon, "Kierkegaard's Stages and *A Brunt-out Case*", *Review of English Literature*, 3 (1962), 99.
197. *A Burnt-out Case*, p. 82.
198. *Ibid.*, p. 199. 199. *Ibid.* 200. *Ibid.*
201. *The Plague*, p. 203.
202. *Ibid.*, p. 107. 203. *Ibid.*, p. 136.
204. *A Burnt-out Case*, p. 122.
205. *Ibid.*, p. 122. 206. *Ibid.*, p. 46. 207. *Ibid.*, p. 135.
208. *Ibid.*, p. 51.
209. *Lord Jim*, p. 297.
210. *A Burnt-out Case*, p. 57.
211. *Ibid.*, p. 186. 212. *Ibid.*, p. 193.
213. Samuel Beckett, *Murphy* (London: G. Routledge and Co., 1938), A Jupiter Book, Calder and Byrons, 1969, p. 123.

214. *Ibid.*, p. 8. 215. *Ibid.*, p. 76. 216. *Ibid.*, p. 152.
217. *Ibid.*, p. 168.
218. *The Plague*, p. 201.
219. *Ibid.* 220. *Ibid.*, p. 206.
221. *A Burnt-out Case*, p. 192.
222. Quoted in Greene's *A Burnt-out Case*, p. 198.
223. *The Concluding Unscientific Postscript*, p. 387.
224. *A Burnt-out Case*, p. 185.
225. *Ibid.*, p. 196. 226. *Ibid.*, p. 114.
227. Walter Kaufmann, *Existenialism from Dostoyevsky to Sartre* (Cleveland and New York: World Publishing Company, 1956), p. 49.
228. "So far faith is concerned, no proofs are of any help, particularly material proofs." *The Brothers Karamazv*, II, p. 748.
229. "If there is one constant theme in the works of modern novelists and playwrights, it is the depth and persistence of human affliction, and indeed that this affliction scourges most heavily, the sensitive, the loving, the compassionate, so that not to be afflicted is to be less than human." Leslie Paul, "The Writer and the Human Condition," *Kenyon Review*, No. 1, XXIX (January 1967), 37.

CHAPTER THREE

The Existential Humanist

THERE is a marked change in Greene's search of a way in which man can, with dignity, confront a universe which is disjointed, purposeless and absurd on account of the disappearance of age-old values. In his later novels, which reveal his leaning towards the Sartrean brand of existentialism, Greene turns from faith in God to faith in man's own inner self. Sartre's views of "existence" and "essence", the feelings of "nausea", "anguish" and "absurdity" and individual *praxis* appear to be reflected in *The Quiet American*, *The Comedians*, *The Honorary Consul* and *The Human Factor*.

There are, according to Sartre, three distinct modes of being: that of the "for-itself" which has to be what it is—*i.e.* which is what it is not and which is not what it is—and that of the "in-itself" which is what it is. Objects have being "in-itself", *en-soi*. People have being "for-itself", *pour-soi*, because consciousness exists for itself. Finally, there is "being-for-others", *pour-autrui*, which means that we all exist in the eyes of other people, and our estimates of ourselves come from what other people think of us. Sartre's *pour-soi*, "whose existence precedes essence",[1] corresponds to the authentic individual of Kierkegaard and to the *Dasein* of Heidegger. "Existence" means the "here" and "now" of being and "essence" is the "what" of being. The term essence refers to our true nature, the ethical self in Kierkegaard. Man is a free individual in the sense of not being determined. He makes effort for essence in life. The *pour-soi* gets defined in terms of negation and freedom. The *pour-soi* comes into being (exists, emerges) by separating itself from the *en-soi* (in-itself). The *en-soi* has its being in itself, and this is the essential being. The *pour-soi* is free to choose its essence and its being is its freedom. Paradoxically, its freedom is also its lack of being. For Sartre, as for Kierkegaard, there is an inner contradiction in existence.

Sartre maintains that the universe is purposeless, it is neither good nor bad, neither moral nor immoral. The working of the universe is mysterious, so is man's existence. Human life is absurd because "there's nothing, nothing, absolutely no reason for existing".[2] Man, imbued with an existence, *pour-soi,* is engaged in a senseless struggle against forces which can neither be mastered nor comprehended: "We were a heap of existents inconvenienced, embarrassed by ourselves, we hadn't the slightest reason for being there, any of us, each existent, embarrassed, vaguely ill at ease, felt superfluous in relation to the others."[3] He experiences nausea and the sense of absurdity arising from the actual unmanageableness of things and his failure wholly to possess them. The dignity of man lies in his ability to face reality in all its senselessness: to accept it freely, without fear, without illusions. In full awareness of the absurd, Sartre's *pour-soi* chooses for all men in choosing for himself. His existential freedom burdens him with a sense of responsibility for others: ". . . man finds himself in an organized situation in which he himself is involved: his choice involves mankind in its entirety, and he cannot avoid choosing."[4]

Sartre's man is nothing else but that which he makes himself and in making himself he assumes responsibility for the entire race. There is no value, nor morality laid down *a priori.* In each case, man must decide alone, without any basis, without guidance. Doubtless, he chooses without reference to any pre-established values but it is unjust to call him capricious. Dostoyevsky writes: "What's to become of men then? Without God and without a future life? Why, in that case, everything is allowed."[5] Everything is indeed permitted in the absence of God, and man is in consequence forlorn, for he cannot find anything to depend upon either within or outside himself. He is seized with fear and anxiety arising from the fact that in making the choice, the *pour-soi* is committing not only himself but in a certain manner all mankind. This anguished responsibility is brought on by the question of whether the concept or image of man he chooses for himself is one that he can choose for all. This sense of responsibility excludes some choices. Sartre observes: "When a man commits himself to anything, fully realizing that he is not only choosing what he will be, but is thereby at the same time a legislator deciding for the whole of mankind—in such a moment a man cannot escape from the sense of complete and profound responsibility."[6]

Sartre's political philosophy seeks to modify Marxims and

change its direction. Marxist concepts are directive principles, indications of tasks; they set problems rather than provide actual concrete truths. In short, they are "regulative ideas".[7] What Sartre proposes, therefore, is the "interiorization" of Marxist thought, and the rendering of it concretely. "Interiorization" seems to mean the same as "making concrete". The fundamental concept upon which Sartre relies for the performance of this proposed rejuvenation of Marxism, is that of *praxis*. *Praxis* is the Greek word for "action" or any purposeful "human activity". The essence of *praxis* is "depassement", *i.e.*, going beyond the existing situation. The notion of *praxis* is connected with that of need *besoin*. It is scarcity *rarite* and the determination to overcome it, which motivates individual human *praxis*. *Praxis* is based in need, "is born of need".[8]

Material obstacles which confront men totalize them into groups. The group emerges out of the collective (the merely serial) when men band together to bring about a change, to revolt against the practico-inert. A new group emerges in relation to an already existing group. In explaining how this comes about, Sartre resorts to the concept of the "third man", a concept developed out of "look"[9] of his earlier thought in *Being and Nothingness*. The "third man" is the observer who understands the workers he is watching and comprehends their *praxis* and freely becomes acting subject, himself a centre of totalization. Such a man becomes a centre of "synthesis", a centre of action determined by a synthetic objective. The "group in fusion"—fusion of many individuals making the same choice, however, can either lapse back into seriality or move on to being a stable "group". The two cementing factors which bring about the latter are the "oath" and "threat" or "fear". Whatever fraternity be founded in the group, is based on fear. The later evolution of the group makes of it an institution and finally the bureaucracy. By this time individual freedom has become alienated and inertia has reappeared. Thus Sartre tries to graft on to a Marxist framework a fragment of liberal ideology, the belief in the efficacy of individual initiative. The attempt is brave, but the result is not very successful.

The Quiet American is Greene's first secular novel in which "religion plays little or no part".[10] Here Greene presents the problem of existence and essence and shows the significance of free existence deciding essence. Like many other novels of Greene, the present novel has emerged from his personal experience as the correspondent of *Life* and the *London Sunday Times* in Indo-China in the fifties, where he stayed "every winter for four years to watch a war".[11] The Indo-China of the novel is torn by factions: the pro-Western Government at Saigon, underground Communist cells in the south, Chinese Communists on the northern border, war-lords like General "The" in both the areas, religious groups that might ferment troubles at any time, Catholics practising a policy of *laissez-faire* with regard to the Communists, the "third force" breaking the deadlock between Colonialism and Communism. As the country is at war, there is lawlessness. A man is suddenly and inexplicably lost to his family and either he joins the Communists or is enlisted in one of the private armies flourishing round Saigon—"the Hoa-Haos or the Caodists or General The"[12] or he is imprisoned. The private armies sell their services for money or revenge—there is nothing picturesque in treachery and distrust. General "The", the Caodist chief of staff, fights "both sides, the French, the Communists".[13] Wherever one goes, one finds pain and suffering—"a strange poor population frightened, cold, starving. . . ."[14] The setting insists on the meaninglesseness of human condition. Unable to comprehend life and its complexity, Fowler, Greene's protagonist in the present novel, feels utterly disgusted: "Wouldn't we all do better not trying to understand, accepting the fact that no human being will ever understand another, not a wife a husband, a lover a mistress, nor a parent a child? Perhaps that's why men have invented God—a being capable of understanding."[15] This calls to mind the statement of Kolya in *The Brothers Karamazov*, II: "God is only a hypothesis but—I admit that he is necessary for—for order—for world order and so on, and that if there were no God he'd have to be invented."[16]

An ardent champion of the individual, Graham Greene appears to be attracted towards individual's freedom of choice or his engagement which lies at the heart of Sartrean existentialism. In Sartre freedom is the human reality—"there is no determinism—man is free, man is freedom".[17] There is no universal nature or essence according to which man might pattern his action and conduct. Fowler is a highly individualized character. A man full of self-pity and melancholy, Fowler is fully aware of his own wretchedness. Like Minty of the *England Made Me*, he drinks, scamps work and is an exile without ambition. In full knowledge of the prevailing situation of Indo-China, he decides not to get himself involved in the political struggle between Colonialists and Communists, because politics do not interest him. Moreover, his attitude of detachment results from a sense of nausea he feels towards the prevailing human condition: "It had been an article of my creed. The human condition being what it was, let them fight, let them love, let them murder, I would not be involved."[18] A man without values and without fidelities except to himself, he is so shrunken in his capacity to believe in public causes and ideals as to be willing to settle for his girl and opium pipe without asking anything more. Deeply concerned with his personal freedom, Fowler is against committing himself either to Communists or to Colonialists supported by Americans because commitment to anything except one's own self means limitation and sacrifice of freedom. Like the existentialists, Fowler hates Communism as it deprives individuals of their freedom to think for themselves and forces them "to believe what they are told".[19] He also condemns America and all that it stands for and it stands for the idea of progress that has a dehumanizing effect on man. He dislikes Americans with their "private stores of Coca-Cola and their portable hospitals and their too wide cars."[20] Fowler seems to be of the view that Americans are too naive to be of any assistance in international situation. His attitude towards the Communists as well as to the Americans seems to reflect Greene's own hatred for Communism which is hostile to individual freedom and his antipathy towards America which stands for present industrialized civilization in which the individual has no place. Fowler is proud of being "de'gagé, the reporter, not the leader writer".[21] He wishes to report what he sees and resents the term: correspondent because it implies action—"even an opinion is a kind of action".[22]

Like Sartre's *pour-soi*, Fowler is aware of a sense of "nothingness". Having no belief in the permanence of life, he is always "afraid of losing happiness".[23] Death, for him, is far more certain than God. Death is the only absolute value in his world. With death the nightmare of a future of boredom and indifference ends: "Lose life and one would lose nothing again for ever."[24]

As in public life, Fowler is uninvolved in private life. A man without any moral scruple, he picks up women and deserts them and feels no attachment to them: "his truth is always temporary."[25] He needs Phoung, his present mistress, because she gives him physical comfort, prepares his opium pipe and drives away the loneliness of his declining years. Neither he feels any responsibility for her nor does he care for "her damned interests".[26]

Greene, like Sartre, lays stress on the need for the individual to be consciously involved, to belong, to be éngagé. He points out that man acts not in a socio-personal vacuum, but rather in a context of concrete situation in which he himself is necessarily involved. Captain Trouin remarks: "It's not a matter of reason or justice. We all get involved in a moment of emotion and then we cannot get out."[27] Fowler protests too much but is unable to refrain from taking sides for ever. A man of deep human awareness, his chief wish is to be at ease and he cannot be at ease "if someone else is in pain, visibly audibly or tactually".[28] He feels terribly shocked at the sight of innocent deaths in the bomb explosion. Like the Whisky-Priest and Scobie, he is sensitive to the suffering of children. "The legless torso"[29] twitching "like a chicken which has lost its head"[30] and the mutilated baby "on its mother's lap"[31] always haunt his mind and the cries of the young soldier mortally wounded by the Viet-Minh brings home to Fowler his own responsibility for suffering: "I was responsible for that voice crying in the dark. I had prided myself on detachment, on not belonging to this war, but those wounds had been inflicted by me just as though I had used the sten."[32]

His hatred for war and his pity for its victims lead him to action which is inconsistent with his chosen role of a non-participating spectator. He enters into a pact with a local Communist and contrives the murder of Pyle, the quiet American, so as to prevent the damage done by his good-will programme. He offers an interesting parallel to Sartre's hero of *Iron in the Soul*, the school-master Mathieu, who spends nine boring months first in the pine woods and later among the vineyards so as to avoid war. A man without "enough courage to make anyone miserable",[33] Mathieu is shaken by the unbearable sight of the terror of war and decides one fine day to get involved. Fowler's action is not political, it is rather personal and comes out of his entire psychic history. Sex is rarely a part of basic motivation in existential literature. Greene's Fowler also desires to get back Phoung not for the satisfaction of sex but for company in old age. At the present stage of his life "sex is not the problem so much as old age and death."[34] Lawrence Lerner appears to be in the wrong when he says, "Fowler is jealous of Pyle who stole his girl."[35] Revenge too is never the cause for his being concerned in Pyle's murder, as it is evident from Pyle's book *The Role of the West* lying on his shelf—"One does not take one's enemy's book as a souvenir."[36] Actually his humanity and the sense of responsibility for the afflicted accentuate his anguish and longing for peace. As it has been cited earlier, he admits that his peace depends upon the peace of others. Thus Fowler's participation in the human situation is caused by his deep human love.

In Sartre's system, individual freedom has another side and this is anguish. Anguish is rooted in the awareness of each human being that his choice and action involve not only himself but all men. Sartre says: "I am thus responsible for myself and all men and I am creating a certain image of man as I would have him to be. In fashioning myself I fashion man."[37] As man's freedom is complete and profound, there is nothing to assure him that he is on the right track. He suffers from existential anguish and forlornness. Sartre says: "In anguish . . . We apprehend our choice . . . *i.e.*, ourselves as unjustifiable."[38]

Fowler reflects the existential mood of anguish and despair at the novel's end. Some critics think that Fowler is sorry for his act of betrayal and repents when he says, "I wished there existed someone to whom I could say that I was sorry."[39] To David Lodge Fowler's involvement fills him "with a sense of guilt for whom his cynicism provides no relief".[40] Actually Fowler does not repent nor does he wish to undo what he has done. He feels no remorse for his action; rather a sort of satisfaction accompanies his judgment when he says, "Everything had gone right with me since he had died."[41] Fowler, rather, suffers from self-contradiction—"*mauvaise foi*".[42] His sense of affliction goes very deep when he finds his position with regard to Phoung unjustifiable: "Perhaps she would never know security; what right had I to value her less than the dead bodies in the square? Suffering is not increased by numbers: one body can contain all the suffering the world can feel. I had judged like a journalist in terms of quantity . . . I had become as engagé as Pyle."[43] Fowler's personal freedom which inspires a sense of responsibility for others is an existential feature. His existential commitment, without the limited loyalty to any group or organization, brings him close to Conrad's hero of *Victory*, "the wandering, drifting, unattached Heyst"[44] who wants "to drift without ever catching on to anything".[45] Both Fowler and Heyst are fundamentally unengaged souls who become conscious of the importance of human act in full awareness of themselves and the concrete situations they are set in.

In a direct contrast to Fowler stands Pyle, an agent of the American Economic Mission, who believes in commitment and who thinks that there must be something one must believe in because "Nobody can go on living without some belief."[46] Absorbed in the dilemmas of democracy and the responsibilities of the West he is committed "to do good, not to any individual person but to a country, a continent, a world".[47] With "his idealism, his half-baked ideas founded on the works of York Harding,"[48] a diplomatic correspondent, Pyle associates himself with the creation of a "Third Force" to save the East from Communism. Though Pyle is good at heart and means well, his noble intentions are fruitless on account of his lack of understanding. Pyle's efforts are debased and misdirected by lack of his experience. Motivated by abstractions and incompetent to assess the real situation, he is mixed up in under-cover activities which result in bombing a public square in which most of the casualties are women and children. Pyle's loyalty to the "Third Force" and its graphic abstractions deprive him of his existential freedom and fossilize his heart. He is appallingly ignorant, callow and unimaginative and he understands nothing except what he has heard in a lecture-hall or read in a book. The pitiable sights of the war-casualties do not move his heart and when he sees a dead body, he does not "even see the wounds".[49] Even in his personal life, he is led by empty ideals. He wants to win Phoung by offering her security and respect not love. He thinks that his money ("about fifty thousand dollars"),[50] he will inherit from his parents and his "good health" and his "blood group"[51] will help him to win Phoung. After winning Phoung from Fowler he waits for special leave to go home and celebrate his marriage in the presence of his parents. He is thus loyal to the past customs and systems and disloyal to his own real self. He rescues Fowler, who is hurt and who is limping at the risk of his own life not out of love and sympathy for Fowler in misery but because he "couldn't have faced Phoung".[52] These are just "heroics" to win Phoung.

On account of his love of abstractions, Pyle fails to develop- his potential for self-actualization and accepts a pattern of life that makes him the instrument of circumstances. He is Sartre's *en-soi* who escapes being responsible for himself and whose own real self remains unrealized. As the intellect and not the heart provides the motive power for his action, he is incapable of emotional response, *i.e.*, a living response.

"The Third Force" and other groups that Greene has described in the book, emerge in the manner in which a new group emerges in Sartre. The formation of a new group in Sartre is based on "us-object-experience" exemplified in a crowd or in the consciousness of class-suppression. A third man becomes a centre of totalization. Greene condemns the groups, like the "Third Force" which emerge on the grounds of ideology. Criticizing the "Third Force" he remarks: "Harding wrote about a third force. Pyle formed one—a shoddy little bandit with two thousand men and a couple of tame tigers. He got mixed up."[53] Greene condemns the group which people join motivated by ideology and not by need. Greene does not appear to be interested in projects and plans which are not given shape or form either because their utopian character condemns them to remain a dream, or because the vicissitudes of the practical revolutionary process force them to be modified or abandoned altogether. Greene insists on the importance of individual's initiative inspired by need or scarcity: "They don't want Communism. They want enough rice . . . they don't want to be shot at. They want one day to be much the same as another. They don't want our white skins around telling them what they want."[54]

Through Fowler and Pyle, Greene seeks to illustrate two modes of action—action rising from man's existential freedom and action inspired by abstract ideals and principles. He examines the issues of involvement and non-involvement and shows that man's concern for personal freedom leading to his responsibility for others is superior to his involvement in politics inspired by his abstract ideological conviction. Greene stresses the significance of man's existential commitment and the irrelevance of idealism uninformed by experience. He, like Sartre, is not so much interested in plans and proposals, however good they may be, as in the primacy of action, *praxis* action that is concrete immediate and is directed towards the individual rather than action addressed to an end which is ambiguous.

The Comedians is Greene's second novel to study the problems of existence and essence. The novel, largely set in Haity, a shabby land of "fear and frustration",[55] insists on the contemporary chaotic life. Through the setting, Greene renders the total vision of gloom. The inhabitants of Haity, ruled over by Papa Doc and his Tontons Macoute, the secret police, suffer from poverty and exploitation. In the unjust and corrupt social political set-up where "The Tontons

Macoute are the only law",[56] people are gripped with a sense of uncertainty and insecurity. None but the chief of police, the head of the Tontons Macoute and the commander of the palace guard have "any permanence".[57] In this disorderly world, houses are burnt with men and their property, innocent men are arrested and imprisoned without any valid grounds and funerals are interrupted. Haity is not "an exception in a sane world",[58] it is rather "a small slice of everyday taken at random".[59] The Sartrean, self-evident, palpable and unredeemable evil of Haity emphasizes the nightmarish nature of modern life.

"The figure of displaced person", says Walter Allen, "can, of course, be taken as a symbol of man's essential situation on this earth."[60] Jones and Brown, who are the uncommitted, are the displaced persons in this fundamental sense. Jones, the self-advertised adventurer and the arch-comedian, is a beach-comber. Out of the two categories of people, shady and respectable—"tarts" and "toffs", he is a "tart" without "a settled job or a good income".[61] All he wants out of life is to make a future, to build a "sahib house"[62] on a desert island. He is accidentally entrapped to lead the rebels in the mountains. Having no experience of the battle-field and suddenly finding himself close to violent death, he gives up his comic mask and feels the need of confessing all his lies and swindlings. Now he understands "why people want to confess. Death's a bloody serious affair".[63] In the moment before death a man confesses to anyone not necessarily to a priest or God. We are reminded of Camus's hero of *The Fall*, who thinks: "One could not die without having confessed all one's lies. Not to God or His representatives, ...No, it was a matter of confessing to men, to a friend, to a beloved woman."[64] Though Jones is only concerned with earning his living in Haity and is least interested in the local events, he appears to have a vague feeling of dislike for the corrupt dictatorial regime and a sense of human love. His agreement with the bloody dictator "means a fortune",[65] nevertheless, his attempt to deceive Papa Doc, who is a terror for the people, may be counted as resistance: "He was risking a lot when he tried to swindle Papa Doc. Don't underrate him,"[66] says Dr. Magiot. He returns his gratitude to Martha for sheltering him by bringing into her house a kind of domesticity. His stories of adventure amuse Martha who suffers from a terrible feeling of loneliness in her house. She has been happy having Jones in her house "hearing people laugh at his bad jokes...."[67] The horror of death does not shake his promise to guide the rebels. Though his own life is in peril, he does not betray his friends, he rather feels respect for the committed. Young Philipot offers him a loving tribute: "He was a wonderful man. With him we began to learn, but he did not have enough time. The men loved him. He made them laugh."[68] Thus Jones, though apparently shady, is really a man who can make people laugh and who can share their sorrows.

Brown, the narrator of the story, is another comedian who seeks to remain uninvolved. Born in Monaco, that is almost the same as being "a citizen of nowhere",[69] brought up by Jesuits, a lapsed Catholic speculator, Brown values his present life more highly than "a future empty of promise".[70] He is intelligent enough to know his way of life—that of a happy-go-lucky comedian. He feels that he can play only comic roles: "Life was a comedy, not the tragedy for which I was prepared".[71] He chooses to wear the comic mask in full awareness of the absurd whlch is inescapable: "The situation isn't abnormal. It belongs to human life. Cruelty's like searchlight. It sweeps from one spot to another. We only escape it for a time."[72] The notion of role-playing has parallels in existential writing. Sartre's Roquentin wants to act because "on the stage it must be possible to obtain perfect moments".[73]

Like Fowler of *The Quiet American*, Brown seeks to attain total detachment in public as well as in private life. Though full of admiration for the dedicated, the Doctor Magiots and Mr. Smiths for their courage and integrity, for their fidelity to a cause, he is too wise to assume that commitment is a good *per se*. He conquers the temptation of sharing the security of a religious creed or a political faith and defends the freedom of the rootless and the faithless who "have chosen nothing except to go on living, rolled round on Earth's diurnal course, with rocks and stones and trees".[74] He anticipates Dr. Plarr of *The Honorary Consul* when he thinks himself to be fit for "the world of comedy and not of tragedy".[75] Brown is unwilling to renounce his personal freedom by committing himself to any belief as "it's a limitation to believe".[76] In his choice of a life of freedom he bears a close resemblance to Sartre's hero Mathieu who is unwilling to join Communism in spite of the persuasion of Mr. Brunet. He reminds us of Conrad's Razumov of *Under Western Eyes*, who refuses to belong to any group or organization and acts in sincerity to his own self. Brown's peculiar intellectual awareness links him to Dostoyevksy's underground hero who openly condemns active life in the midst of life's absurdity: "It is best to do nothing, The best thing is conscious inertia."[77] In the face of the absurd, only the stupids are valiant. "Every decent man in this age is, and must be, a coward and a slave. That is his normal condition. . .only donkeys and mules make a show of bravery. . . ."[78] The comedy in Greene conveys a similar feeling and depth of focus. Brown is aware of himself, his role, his way of life and the loss of normal human feelings. Smiths and Doctor Magiot and the rebels are the prisoners of innocence—"donkeys and mules". They scarifice themselves meaninglessly. Like Pyle of *The Quiet American*, they have fantastic attitude to life and in consequence are impervious to reality. Brown, on the contrary, is able to exist without the aid of heroic light and any positive ideals. God to him is just "an authoritative practical joker"[79] driving human beings "towards the extreme point of comedy".[80] God is no longer the conventional, omnipotent God inspiring human beings to lay down their lives for the higher ideals of life. The Whisky-Priest, Scobie and Sarah believed in God and were prepared for tragedy. We note a change with Bendrix, who in a state of exhaustion prays to God to leave him "alone for ever".[81] His secular outlook is challenged by the divine order. But in Fowler and Querry the challenge is gradually weaker and more oblique. The castle of sand that his heroes have been trying to build by affirming to the religious creed, finally crumbles. David Lodge aptly points out: "Greene's progress from fiction based on a tragic conflict between human and divine values to fiction conceived in terms of comedy and irony in which the possibility of religious faith has all been retreated out of sight in the anarchic confusion of human behaviour."[82] Brown is the typical Greene hero who faces the truth about human existence in all its starkness. Awareness of the fundamental absurdity, according to Camus, is the measure of man's achievement in terms of knowledge. Camus says: "No code of ethics and no effort are justifiable *a priori* in the face of cruel mathematics that command our condition."[83] Greene seems to envision a similar spiritual condition in the present novel. Brown, like the absurd man defined by Camus, shuns all absolutes and lives solely "without appeal".[84] He is actually "the anti-hero",[85] a term used in modern fiction for a ragged assembly of victims—the fool, the clown, the hipster, the criminal, the poor sod, the freak, the outsider, the rebel without a cause.

Brown, though unwilling to be drawn into the vortex of

politics and utterly nauseated with the corruption of power, has a feeble sense of responsibility. As Fowler is drawn into action by his humanity and concern for the suffering, Brown is led into political intrigues through his connection with Jones and Young Philipot. His relation to Jones is a sign of human love. Though a mere chance acquaintance, Jones becomes for him "an unknown brother".[86] Both of them, Brown says, are bastards "thrown into the water to sink or swim".[87] They are both individuals of illegitimate birth. In this age of incongruities and objective uncertainty "the bastard"[88] becomes the truly representative figure of modern man. Knowing well that "anyone who touches Major Jones is in trouble",[89] Brown helps Jones to take shelter in the house of his German mistress out of a sense of sharing another's sorrow. While laying the trap for Jones, he is no doubt driven by jealousy for Jones's ability to make people laugh and his apparent intimacy with Martha, nevertheless, there appears to be another motive in the depth, that is, his concern for the fate of the rebels. Jones, he thinks, would be a competent leader the rebels are in need of. But he is shocked to discover the reality about him and with deep regret he utters, "I can't smuggle you back".[90] His affair with Martha too is suggestive of his human concern. In the beginning he is drawn to her purely for the satisfaction of sex—"a bit of lust and a bit of curiosity"[91] is all he feels for her. Not conditioned by sexuality, his love-affair with Martha is needed just to balance the fear and boredom of life. It lacks maturity and permanence. As his first love-affair with his instructress fifteen years older than himself ended without pain or regret, so he parts from Martha without the pain of separation. His relation to her was conditioned by her filial affection. Brown says: ". . . it was not Martha's love for me which held me . . . it was her blind unselfish attachment to her child."[92] Eventually he begins to love Martha's fat husband for whom he bore hatred and sees no reason why "Martha should not like him too".[93] He also feels sympathy for Martha's fat boy and wonders why in the past "he had found him so detestable".[94] His human love seems to let him involved in the political action which threatens his security. In the teeth of bullets, Brown crosses over the border and like Sartre's hero accepts his worsening situation. He agrees to become an undertaker.

In contrast to these characters, Greene sets those who are committed to an ideal or to a system. Mr. and Mrs. Smith, the good

Pelagian Americans, are committed to an ideal of vegetarianism. Mr. Smith, the ludicrous idealist, thinks in big terms—"mankind, justice, human happiness"[95]—and believes that vegetarianism will eliminate acidity and will help people to grow conscientious. People, cured of acidity, will refuse to have innocent animals butchered for pleasure and in course of time turn away "in horror from killing a fellowman".[96] The sight of poverty, exploitation, terror pervading entire Haitian life and the evidence of police authoritarianism—the arrest and imprisonment of Jones by Tontons and the manhandling of his wife for interfering in their kidnapping of the dead body of Doctor Philipot, the crippled beggars selling old dirty stamps near the post office—do not shake his faith and enthusiasm: "The dream was intact . . . Reality did not touch him, even the scene in the post office has not sullied his vision."[97] The dreamy, well-wishing and unimaginative Mr. Smith calls to mind Pyle, the innocent American of *The Quiet American.* But unlike Pyle, Mr. Smith is disillusioned and "despairs of everything here".[98] The pitiable sight of the homeless crippled artist, approaching him for help, opens "his eyes"[99] and he realizes that people are not "ripe here for vegetarianism".[100] The corruption and violence, misery and poverty prove too much for him and his zeal for vegetarianism is wiped out in Haitian greed.

Dr. Magiot, the negro Communist, is another committed character who "would rather have blood" on his hands "than water like Pilate".[101] He believes "in the future of Communism and in certain economic law".[102] A deep humanist, Doctor Magiot is disgusted with the rule of the dictator and believes in a palace-revolution, "a purge from the people",[103] a mass revolution which will destroy the rule of the autocrat. Suspected of being Castro's agent, he is killed by the police and his desire to see Haity free from evil and corruption does not materialize.

Besides, we have the rebels who are committed to force. The victims of the dictatorship group together making the common choice and use violence so as to bring about a change in the present situation. Young Henry Philipot, who experiences intense misery at an early age, changes his role from that of a comedian to that of a staunch committed guerrilla. Doctor Magiot may be called the "third man", the observer who understands the victims and comprehends their *praxis*. He arranges a leader for the rebels through Brown. Though their prowess wins admiration of the people and probably of Greene too, they are unlikely to cause any appreciable change in the situation. Greene is against "violence".[104] The rebels kill a few Tontons Macoute and then they themselves get killed without bringing about any change in the existing set-up: "Poor souls, they don't know how to fight. They go waving their rifles, if they've got them, at a fortified post. They may be heroes, but they have to learn to live and not to die."[105] Greene's characters, who are committed, suggest that the attempts to fight out evil through techniques of organization prove ineffective. In an evil land, good and harmless cannot be achieved through ideological commitment which is irrelevant and absurd. Projects and proposals most often go berserk because of the utopian elements they harbour or because of the sudden changes in social and political process. The novel presents the two possible modes of life—"the rational and the irrational, misery or gaiety"[106] and points out that commitment to a course of action without direct personal and emotional experience is meaningless and proves disastrous. Commitment is meaningful when it is motivated by deeper personal forces rather than the abstract vision of the future. *The Comedians*, like *The Quiet American*, insists on the significance of man's existential freedom leading to his care and concern for others.

The Honorary Consul, like the novels it follows, *The Quiet American* and *The Comedians*, presents the problem of éngagé and dégagé in the world dominated by political ideologies. The setting in a small seedy Argentinian town and the action concerning the plan of the terrorists to kidnap the American Ambassador going wrong and the arrest of Charley Fortnum, the Honorary Consul, by mistake and Doctor Edurado Plarr's becoming an accessory to the kidnappers' plot—all emphasize that life is gratuitous, irreducible and absurd. Doctor Plarr says: "Nothing is ever what we intend. They didn't mean to kidnap you. I didn't mean to start the child. You would almost think there was a great joker somewhere who likes to give a twist to things."[107] Life is painful and ugly, it is never fully happy and satisfying. Here one must often find "intolerable pain—a child dying of meningitis"[108] and the police stations where things like the cutting of Aquino's fingers most often happen.

Doctor Plarr, a familiar Greene figure, is the son of a liberal political activist supposed to be dead or in a prison in Paraguay. He feels grief for his father and "a sense of guilt because of his own safety and comfort".[109] Like his father, Dr. Plarr is full of compassion for the poor and in the barrio of the poor he is aware of doing something his father would like to see but when he is with rich patients, he feels as though he has left his father's friends "to help his enemies".[110] Apart from what he feels for his father and the poor, his father's favourites, Dr. Plarr is an emotionally deficient man. Without ties or loyalties or even very strong desires, Dr. Plarr is an exhausted man, "a cold fish"[111] in an absurd and sterile society. Like Fowler and Brown, he is a passive observer of life, incapable of love, political action, religious belief or indeed anything else except adultery with his patients. Deeply aware of life's absurdity, he longs to tell Saavedra who is writing "a political novel of lasting value"[112] that "Life is not noble or dignified. . . Nothing is ineluctable. Life has surprises. Life is absurd."[113]

In utter disgust with life's absurdity, Dr. Plarr cultivates a deliberate detachment in private as well as in public life. He fears caring because "caring is the only dangerous thing".[114] There is no sentimental relic in his apartment—not even a photograph. It is "as bare and truthful—almost as a police station cell".[115] His experiences with women, including his own mother, have made him deeply suspicious of love which, to him, is just a "comedy of passion"[116] which whores play out for their customers. Comedy means pretence or role-playing. Dr. Plarr sees life as a comedy which means to deny its significance. His attitude of detachment leads him to take sex casually. Love, for him, is a responsibility he wants to avoid at all cost, "a claim which he wouldn't meet, a responsibility he would refuse to accept".[117] During his affairs with several responsive married patients, he tries to avoid the phrase of the theatre "I love you."[118] He is always able to find some other explanation of his behaviour with women—"loneliness, pride, physical desire or even a simple sense of curiosity"[119] and bears a close resemblance to Brown of *The Comedians*. Even his affair with Clara begins clumsily. In his relations with Clara, he is always concerned about his own freedom and takes her to bed to free himself of his obsession. He seduces her out of cold curiosity and thinks with relief after the act, "this is the end of my obsession. . . I'm a free man again."[120] He advises abortion when she is pregnant. Clara informs Fortnum that Dr. Plarr wanted her "to kill the baby. . . He really wanted it."[121] Dr. Plarr debunks *machismo*[122] as an irrational concept, which has "ceased to exist except in the romantic imagination of writers like Saavedra".[123]

Honour, as Dr. Plarr thinks, means nothing to the starving who are engaged in a more serious fight for survival. He is filled with anger and hatred for God, "that horror up there sitting in the clouds of heaven"[124] who produces abortion and allows things like the birth of a child "without hands and feet... poor bloody torso".[125]

Fortnum, like Captain Druin in *The Quiet American*, remarks: "People do get caught up by love... sooner or later."[126] In the course of the novel, Plarr finds himself becoming involved. Though he refuses to recognize his emotion as love, this disturbing passion makes its appearance and an unaccustomed tenderness replaces lust and his sense of triumph and he feels sad and depressed after the sexual act: "He felt no lust... he felt no sense of triumph... There seemed to be no point in playing the game since now he knew what moves he had to make to win. The moves were sympathy, tenderness, quiet, the counterfeiting of love."[127] The complacency of Charley Fortnum, whose love for his wife survives betrayal, is embarrassing to Plarr and stirs jealousy which is the sign of love. However, to Dr. Plarr, love is no more than "a question of semantics".[128] Plagued with jealousy, he observes: "That stupid banal word love. It's never meant anything to me. Like the word God. I know how to fuck—I don't know how to love. Poor drunken Charley Fortnum wins the game."[129] The admission of defeat confirms his involvement and guilt. Dr. Plarr, who has been afraid of caring and anxious to avoid responsibility, comes to loving, caring and feeling guilty.

Greene seems to be interested in the interaction of the private and public lives of his characters. Private involvement is linked with political involvement. Dr. Plarr, like Fowler, takes no interest in politics nor is he a Communist. He finds Marx "unreadable. Like most economics."[130] Though unwilling to be mixed up with the plot of the terrorists because he doubts the efficacy of an organization, he is drawn to the centre of the scheme by his personal motives. His getting involved in the plot, in the first place, is "a mark of friendship".[131] Moreover, he hopes that his father will be freed as a part of the ransom if he is still alive in one of "the General's goals".[132] His love for Clara, a teenage ex-whore, at present four months pregnant by Plarr, is another motive for his action: "And besides, there is Fortnum. I can't help feeling responsible a bit for him. He's not a patient of mine, but Mrs. Fortnum is."[133] Though he is reluctant to act—("let this comedy end in comedy. None of us are suited to tragedy"[134])—and one of the motives for action is lost with the confirmed news of his father's death, his sense of humanity and responsibility is so deeply shaken that it is not possible for him to retrace his steps from the abyss of involvement. He feels a tie with the child, who is no longer "a useless part of Clara like her appendix, perhaps a diseased appendix which ought to be removed".[135] He now grows very anxious to make "some sort of arrangement for it".[136] Unshaken by the thought of his own death, out of compassion for Clara and the child, he walks out of the rebel hide-away to death in an attempt to save Fortnum, who "would make a better father"[137] than himself. His decision to face the situation instead of shifting it to "God"[138] calls to mind Dr. Rieux of Camus who would not believe in God and "cease curing the sick".[139] Dr. Plarr embraces death out of concern for others. Thus his personal commitment leads him to connive with the revolutionaries whose political commitment is alien to him.

Charley Fortnum, the title character of the novel, an old man of sixty, is one of Greene's seedy characters. Lonely, melancholy and full of self-pity, steeped in alcohol and married to a former whore, Fortnum is merely concerned with life here and now. Not even a "proper Consul"[140] whose kidnapping produces a ripple in the international relations, he is significant to Greene because of his existential concern with life. Having no faith in life "afterwards", he simply likes to live another ten years at his camp "watching the little bastard grow".[141] He emerges a tragic figure who resolves the balance by putting the deaths of Dr. Plarr and Rivas in the right perspectives. His feeling of "an odd kinship with that preist"[142] who intended to kill him and "a pang of pain"[143] for Plarr who is young enough to be his son confirm his human love. Fortnum's capacity for love is a part of his humanity. The humanity of the people, however depraved they may be, is one of Greene's main concerns. The situation of the novel reminds us of Sartre's characters of *The Age of Reason*. Mathieu, like Plarr, is obsessed with a desire for personal freedom and tries to raise money for the abortion of Marcelle who is pregnant by him. "He's a wash-out, he's a rotter."[144] He sleeps with all and sundry to escape from life ". . .he does not care much about his girl. He stays with her because he must sleep with someone."[145] Hearing that Marcelle is pregnant, he considers himself pledged to her by ties as strict as those of marriage, he decides "on an operation for abortion under the best possible conditions".[146]

Fortnum also reminds us of Sartre's Daniel, who is a homosexual and, like Fortnum, an inadequate performer in bed. Like Fortnum, Daniel too is willing to name the child after its actual father—"If it's a boy, we will call him Mathieu."[147] His decision to marry the girl and keep the child is the mark of pure human love.

Graham Greene sets his characters in juxtaposition to set off one another. As Pyle to Fowler and Dr. Magiot to Jones and Brown, Father Rivas stands as contrasted to Dr Plarr. Nauseated with the absurdity and pervasive injustice of life, Father Rivas has been aspiring since childhood to become a fearless *abogado* to defend the poor and the innocent. He joins the church as a priest. But he finds it hard to come to terms with the God-abandoned world of suffering and cruelty. The irrelevance of the teachings of the church to the problems of the present-day world—("You learn the rules and find they do not apply to any human cause"[148]) –revolts him. He feels ashamed to read to the poor people, "sell and give to the poor" while the old Archbishop is "eating a fine fish from Iguazu and drinking a French wine with the General".[149] Driven by compassion and a sense of justice into rebellion, he leads the terrorist plot against General Stroessner. Though alienated by his loyalty to El Tiger, he asserts his humanity when he meets his death in an attempt to save Dr. Plarr—"I thought you might need me".[150] His self-sacrificial death reminds us of the Whisky-Priest of *The Power and the Glory*. The priests in both the novels die as criminals in the eyes of the State and renegades in the eyes of the church. *The Honorary Consul* may be seen as a companion piece to *The Power and the Glory*. The priest in *The Power and the Glory* overcomes his cowardice and preserves his faith despite the religious persecution of a military dictatorship. The priest of *The Honorary Consul* becomes a revolutionary and abandons the church which has entered into an alliance with a right-wing military dictatorship.

Father Rivas, Aquino, Pablo and other revolutionaries, motivated by the need to bring about a change in the present unjust and unhappy situation under General Stroessner, form a group under El Tiger, "The one who gives the orders".[151] Their kidnapping of the Honorary Consul and trying to blackmail the people in power comes very close to Sartre's concept of *praxis* and the "group in fusion". The members are human beings who have freely chosen to work upon the orders of their leaders. But their freedom is alienated, they are only instruments, carrying out instructions. Father Rivas feels sympathy for Fortnum and sees that the blackmail has failed, still he cannot let Fortnum get off as he is "a man under orders".[152] The blackmail does not succeed, Fortnum is rescued by the army.

Thus *The Honorary Consul*, like *The Quiet American* and *The Comedians*, is mainly concerned with man's existential freedom inspiring a sense of responsibility for others and it records Greene's distrust in plans and projects. Rivas's political commitment is subsidiary to Plarr's existential commitment. The author points out that man's involvement in the extremes of conduct without any direct emotional or personal experience turns out villainous. Dr. Plarr's involvement and death emphasize the significance of action which is concrete and immediate and which is directed towards the individuals. Dr. Plarr is Sartre's *pour-soi*, for-itself which is what it is not and which is not what it is, his own experience and personal concern and not abstract ideals inspire his commitments. The novel's main focus is on human love, its perils and its values. The unusual tenderness between the incongruous lovers with which the novel closes, suggests that the ideal of human love, though prone to distortion, is potentially of the highest value. Human problems can be solved through the respect, concern and commitment which form the basis of the philosophy of humanism which the present novel embodies. This view places Greene in the company of Sartre who defines man only in relation to his "commitments".[153]

The Human Factor, Greene's latest novel to date, thoroughly explores the tragic mess of contemporary life. The themes of man's deep feeling of boredom, anxiety and nausea arising from secret codes and the bureaucracy and the problem of the committed and the uncommitted in confrontation with the absurd are emphatically projected in the present novel. Greene pours scorn on the evils of the present industrialized Western civilization that has created a widespread "feelings of ressentiment"[154] and a problem of man's self-awareness. The unclean bureaucracy, which is the characteristic of modern life, has dehumanizing influence upon the individuals and produces heartless men who can shamelessly justify even the murder of an innocent man and captives of society existing in painless obedience. There is a decrease in the level of responsibility people feel for one another and human relationships have sunk to the level of market values. Man is gripped by an anxious sense of being left alone in the midst of nothingness. Love is "a total risk"[155] one fears to speak of to others because it invites danger: "Love and hate are both dangerous . . . A man in love walks through the world like an anarchist, carrying a time bomb".[156] The worst effect is that most people accept their conditions and become insensitive to their captivity to the system. Anyone who attempts to revolt becomes the victim of bitter *ressentiment* and the full force of institution, legal and penal, is brought to bear upon him. The characters of the present novel very well illustrate this point of view. Most of these characters experience a moment of uneasy relation between personal and professional self. They suffer from an invisible inner panic that has nothing to do with competence and self-confidence. This is the sense of incongruity that rises from the confusion between social and personal confirmation.

Maurice Castle, the British Secret Service Agent, whose surname suggests the lonely and guarded aspects of his profession and his character, suffers from anxiety and restlessness. A man of regular habits, very cautious about money and drink, competent at the office, "Dullish man, first class, of course, with files . . . careful and scrupulous",[157] happily married to Sarah, a black South African woman with a young son from a previous lover, a rare instance of marital fulfilment in Greene's fiction, feels ill at ease for security risks. A double agent leaking out secrets of his office to the Russians so as to repay his debt to the Communist friend Carson, who helped him to escape from the racists of Pretoria, Castle apprehends the detection of his role as a double agent. He is worried about what will happen to both of them if something happens to him and "something does always happen in the end, doesn't it?"[158] Like Heidegger's *Dasein*, he is always seized with the fear of the uncertain. He suffers from the feeling of separation from the people around him and his life at the office, where he is supposed to work with his "mouth shut like a criminal",[159] "among surnames and initials",[160] stirs in him a bitter feeling of revulsion. Castle longs to experience a sense of security which he had once felt while he was being carried from his ward in a hospital towards a major operation—"an object on a conveyor belt . . . with no responsibility, to anyone or anything, even to his own body".[161] He always hopes that before long he would move towards death with the same sense that before long he would be released from anxiety for ever. But he never attains that aspired state of for-itself-in-itself and remains angst-ridden till the end. The shocking event of Davis's death for which he is, to a great extent, responsible augments the sense of his guilt and at the end of the tether, like Fowler and Jones, he feels the need of confession. When the Roman Catholic priest, "another victim of loneliness and silence like himself"[162] fails to understand his problem, "begun so many years ago in a strange country",[163] he reveals the mystery of his role to Sarah, confesses to Daintry that Davis is innocent "because I am the leak",[164] and escapes the bureaucratic rigmarole.

Colonel Daintry, the lonely security chief, who is conscientious, silent, restless and who is locked in thoughts, gives "the impression of a prisoner cooped up in a cell".[165] Daintry is another man suffering from a bitter tension rising from professional and personal confirmation. He is estranged from his bitchy wife and only daughter, and having nothing in common with his companions, he feels left out in "the world outside the borders of security".[166] He envies Doctor Percival who is always "at ease with strangers".[167] Daintry, on the other hand, feels nervous in encountering his own wife in the registry office on the occasion of his daughter's wedding. Tired to death "of secrecy and of errors"[168] which are "to be covered up and not admitted",[169] Daintry shows the signs of wanting to be a free man without duties and obligations which "killed his marriage with their secrets".[170] Daintry, the wise policeman, is allowed a humanization similar to Castle's. The kinship between the two goes back to that between the Whisky-Priest and the Lieutenant in *The Power and the Glory*, Castle emerging as a reincarnation of the Priest and Daintry coming close to the good man in a bad job.

Arthur Davis, a colleague of Castle in the British Secret Service, an eccentric bachelor "a bit of a manic depressive"[171] who spends a good deal on port, whisky and his Jaguar, a comic figure right up to the moment of his death, suffers from a deep sense of incongruity in his office. Davis and Daintry, two displaced figures appear like "two emigrants . . . on deck for the same purpose".[172] Terribly bored in the office, he drinks hard to conquer the feeling of boredom: "when I am bored I drink—You are lucky to have Sarah",[173] he says to Castle. His friendship with Castle enables him to get through his work in the office and saves him from "crack up".[174] The feeling of disgust with life reaches its height when he is mistakenly suspected for the leak in his section: "I'm the sort of man who is always found out. And yet I nearly always obey the rules . . . If I take out a report once to read at lunch, I'm spotted."[175] The security risks of the profession induce in him, as in

Castle and Daintry, a bitter sense of annoyance: "what a damn silly profession ours is. You can't trust anyone".[176] His tragic end—[he is mistakenly bumped off by his own side for a security leak]—emphasizes how absurd life is.

Even John Hargreaves, the Head of the British Secret Service, suffers from a feeling of discontent and is inclined to keep himself aloof from his office. Since children would have been a constant trouble, he agreed to remain childless throughout his life and so did not add to his "public responsibilities private responsibilities".[177] He is terribly bored with the office work which always intrudes in spite of his effort to keep the office away. He is troubled by a sense of guilt at Davis's death and regrets having reacted stupidly and left "Pervical in charge of the case".[178] Out of utter disgust for the awfully busy city life, John Hargreaves, a typical inhabitant of modern mechanical world, sometimes wishes if he were "back to Africa".[179] His love for Africa where, according to him, a man gets "to trust an intuition",[180] is a sign of his nausea for the civilized life. This reminds us of Greene's own attraction towards the simple and peaceful life of the African natives. But Hargreaves feels utterly hopeless and helpless too: "One does not expect peace for long in this job. I don't suppose I'd enjoy it any way."[181] John Hargreaves's feeling of restlessnes implies the general feeling of restlessness and unease that man suffers from in modern mechanical busy urban life.

In contrast to the characters who suffer from boredom, anxiety and restlessness, Greene sets those who are unconscious of having a self and who allow themselves to be used as factotum in the cause of bureaucracy. Cornelius Muller, the former hunter of Castle and Sarah, is now a high South African Security Official and liaison for "Uncle Remus".[182] A courteous unflappable professional, he is a craftsman, a cool operator as chilly as the English assassin, Dr. Pervical. A man without prejudices and ideals, Muller is quite untouched by "the torments of any belief, human or religious".[183] A conformist who is ready to receive orders and obey them promptly without question, Muller is absorbed in collective responses and attitudes and allows himself to be swallowed up in "das man". Stripped of his subjectivity, alienated from his authentic self, he is reduced to the status of an ohject *en-soi* in-itself which is what it is.

Dr. Emmanuel Percival, the most unpleasant of the British spies, is a medical man, in charge of the British Secret Service elimination exercises. Like Muller, he is a captive to the system and is unaware of his captivity. Being mixed up with the spying work, he is a bit "out of practice in general medicine"[184] because "security is more important than a correct diagnosis in this outfit".[185] Lost in the vortex of bureaucracy, he sees his duty in abstract terms. Explaining the service code to Daintry, he says: "You haven't been a long time with us, have you, or you'd know how we live in boxes —you know—boxes."[186] A cool devil, incapable of feeling love and pity, he is not troubled by any sense of guilt when the murder of Davis is pinned on him; he rather justifies the act of murder: "He's no loss to the firm, John. He should never have been recruited. He was inefficient and careless and drank too much. He'd have been a problem sooner or later any way."[187]

Thus all except Percival and Muller feel embarrassed and ill at ease in the face of the incongruous in life and anxiously long to transcend the confinements of their conditions. Maurice Castle, the central consciousness of the novel, and Colonel Daintry revolt against the bureaucracy which restricts their freedom and prevents them from living a personal life. Castle is another in the series of morally exhausted protagonists that nominally starts with Querry although traditionally stretches back to Scobie and beyond. He is careful to preserve his autonomy and his passionate desire to be himself drives him to the rejection of every human commitment. Free from ideological affiliations and a man having "no politics",[188] he wants nothing out of life except "a permanent home in a city where he could be accepted as a citizen, as a citizen without any pledge of faith, not the city of God or Marx; but the city called Peace of Mind".[189] Here, as elsewhere, Greene stresses the impossibility of making a separate peace and points out that nobody can escape responsibility by doing nothing, since the world will always catch up. Castle too is drawn into loyalties and attachments and, unlike earlier heroes, he is drawn in willingly. He refuses to remain within his "box" and conspires with Soviet Intelligence, instead of co-operating with Boss, the South African Intelligence System, as instructed by his British superiors. His betrayal is motivated first by his "debt to Carson"[190] and not by ideology: "I've never pretended that I share your faith—I'll never be a Communist."[191] He has a sense of relief for having repaid his debt and asks Boris to drop him because he is doubly dangerous: "Hate's liable to make mistakes. It's as dangerous as love. . . I love too."[192]

In the meanwhile Castle learns about "Operation Uncle

Remus" which involves him for good. From behind his moat of respectability and silence he launches his personal crusade against Western Governments which plan to start a technological revolution in Africa with the help of the latest mining machines. His second betrayal is motivated by "a certain automatic sympathy for Black Africans"[193] and the fear of what "Operation Uncle Remus" might do to the Africans. He has become a "naturalized black".[194] through his marriage with Sarah. He is full of love and sympathy for the people who are engaged in cultivation in the African desert and will strive to defend them: "He would not die fighting for apartheid or for the white race but for so many morgen which he called his own, subject to drought and floods and earthquakes and cattle disease . . . ."[195] Admiring a white farmer in Africa, Castle says to his wife: "He was one of those who will have to die when your people take control . . . I meant of course our people".[196] Thus his personal experience leads Castle to commitment. He parallels Conrad's Razumov of *Under Western Eyes* to whom life is a "dream and fear"[197] and who wants to play his part of a "helpless spectator to the end"[198] and who, like Castle, refuses to commit himself to either the Czarist Government or to the anarchists but whose very neutrality entraps him. He is thrown off his balance by a sudden, unexpected and disastrous blow of fate that is foreign to his usual mode of thought and outside his normal line of behaviour. Razumov writhes because he realizes his human responsibility.

Castle's conscience and experience of Africa inspire him to prefer Communist principles. He is not interested in the abstract Marxist ideals nor does he have "any trust in Marx or Lenin".[199] He rather lives the ideals of Communism, as is evident from his love for the pristine simplicity of the African farmers and his attempt to check the inroads of industrialism into Africa. Through his character Greene, like Sartre, seems to be insisting on the significance of the "interiorization" of Marxist thought.

Thus the novel conveys asense of futility and dispensability which modern man feels in life. Greene's love for the simple and peaceful life of the Africans is a mark of his protest against the flattery, commercialism and the polite corruption of civilization. Like Kurtz of Conrad's *The Heart of Darkness*, who finds a kind of release from the moral restraints of the civilized world in the primitive culture of central Africa, Greene's characters, who have seen the simple peaceful life of the African natives, are capable of sympathy, love and compassion. Castle learns "the age-old lesson that fear and love are indivisible in South Africa".[200] He is the existential hero, the haunted anguished creature of Sartre, a wraith surrounded by the void and forsaken by God. He is absolutely alone and free, creating for himself a personal way of life out of the void of nothingness all round him. Like the non-participating Mathieu of Sartre's novel *The Age of Reason*, Castle is caught in a net of contingencies, coming partly from the sub-conscious levels of his own self, partly from the environment from which he cannot withdraw. Though exiled in Russia and stripped of his family and home, he is reduced to the status of "a man on the dole",[201] living on the gratitude of others which "like love needs to be renewed daily or it's liable to die away",[202] he possesses the existential centre from which to project his vision of the present into the future. His success at getting into telephonic communication with his wife who tells him "to go on hoping"[203] signifies a kind of triumph, however short-lived, over both Russian technology and English surveillance. He thus reminds us of the inability of Beckett's heroes to be nihilists even in a situation of utter helplessness. Vladimir and Estragon in *Waiting For Godot* conclude from the fact of their existence that there must be something for which they are waiting, they are the champions of the doctrine that life must have some meaning even in a manifestly meaningless situation. Greene's hero too embodies the affirmative life-embracing aspect of existentialism rather than its destructive aspect, experiencing new life in relation to phenomena he no longer understands or controls. Through him Greene stresses the significance of discovering the human in the very heart of the bewildering social hierarchy, personal meaning in the midst of the impersonal absurd.

This study of Greene's later novels reveals a close affinity between Greene and Sartre. Man, according to Sartre, finds himself confronted by "two very different modes of action; the one concrete, immediate, but directed towards only one individual; and the other an action addressed to an end infinitely greater, a national collectivity, but for that very reason ambiguous—and it might be frustrated on the way".[204] Greene, like Sartre, points out that in face of the incongruous and absurd in life today, man, convinced of his own worthlessness and degradation, avoids commitment and concerns himself with the private pursuit of happiness, resulting in unconscious and emotional involvement with others. Ideological commitment, being the other alternative, leads to ultimate defeat or death of the person who makes commitment. Greene seems to be suggesting no way out of the modern impasse and his characters, committed as well as uncommitted, meet with anguish, disillusionment, death, defeat or isolation. Pyle, Doctor Magiot, Father Rivas are destroyed. Fowler, Brown and Jones are disillusioned and Maurice Castle is isolated. Brown and Jones perform a slow and tiring journey in order to meet the rebels. Journey has been used right from the days of Homer to symbolize man's spiritual quest. Instead of returning to Ithaca (back home) or the celestial city, Greene's heroes have an overwhelming sense of misery, sordidness and absurdity of human existence. Brown finds himself "on a great plain", there are "no heights and no abysses".[205] Similarly, Jones is tired and cannot find water "among the dry rocks on the flat plain".[206] They represent Greene's stand whose search for meaning leads him to a desert without any prospect of an oasis. Greene's stance implied by his characters comes very close to that of Kafka. He seems to be suggesting like the hero of Kafka's *The Trial* to whom the only sensible thing is "to adapt oneself to existing conditions"[207] and if someone takes it upon oneself to alter the disposition of things around him, he runs "the risk of losing his footing and falling to destruction".[208] Though Greene's characters are disillusioned, destroyed, defeated or isolated, it is rash to conclude that Greene is pessimistic or nihilistic showing the futility of human activity in a chaotic world. His heroes are not good men in the conventional sense—they tell lies, drink, they betray, they commit adultery, they are traitors. It is, however, in the scale of values which the novels set up that the heroes remain right in doing what they have done. Even though life defeats them, they could not have lived it honestly in any other way. In their death, disillusionment or isolation, Greene's heroes, who strive hard for existence, appear to have discovered some values of life like love, nobility, dignity and authenticity. Greene's fiction is a tirade against the establishments as it operates against the individual, binds him with rights and values that are already given and conceals from him his power to blaze his own path. Greene, like Dr. Magiot of *The Comedians*, appears to be full of dislike for the word "Marxist" which "is used so often to describe only a particular economic plan".[209] An advocate of man Greene focuses on the fate of individuals, protests against ideological affiliation and lays bare secret and subtle motivations that impel us all. He insists on man's disloyalty to institutions that threaten his ideals of individualism and humanism. Like Conrad, Greene suggests some kind of action at the individual level and insists on man's care, concern and sympathy for another man arising from his existential experience. Though Greene does not seem to be glorifying the collective *praxis* created by action at the individual level, he vehemently criticizes contemporary man's habit of sinking into separation and isolation and points out that a man must draw his soul out of its isolation and work for some great act of human intercourse based on brotherly love.

Greene's later novels reflect his intense search for a way of life which will preserve the dignity of the individual in a materialistic society. He has travelled a long way from the world of *Brighton Rock* when religious values associated with "good and evil" were asserted to be intrinsically superior to the traditional values of right and wrong. The world which Greene now portrays is one in which the individual's awakening to moral responsibility is seen as fundamental to any life because it gives itself meaning. After a winding and intricate journey that he started with *The Man Within*, he seems to have arrived at a destination.

Notes and References

1. Jean-Paul Sartre, *Existentialism and Humanism*, trans. Philip Mairet (London: Methuen & Co. Ltd., 1948), p. 52.
2. —, *Nausea*, p. 162.
3. *Ibid.*, p. 184.
4. *Existentialism and Humanism*, p. 48.
5. *The Brothers Karamazov*, II, p. 691.
6. *Existentialism and Humanism*, p. 30.
7. Jean-Paul Sartre, *The Problem of Method*, trans. H.E. Barnes (London, 1963), p. 33.
8. *Ibid.*, p. 170.
9. —, *Being and Nothingness*, pp. 340-400.
10. R.W.B. Lewis, "The Fiction of Graham Greene: Between the Horror and the Glory", *The Kenyon Review*, xix (Winter 1957), 56.
11. A.S. Raman, "Chiaroscuro", *The Illustrated Weekly of India*, January 19, 1964, p. 21.
12. Graham Greene, *The Quiet American* (London: William Heinemann Ltd., 1955), Penguin Books, 1973, p. 15.
13. *Ibid.*, p. 25. 14. *Ibid.*, p. 49. 15. *Ibid.*, p. 60.
16. *The Brothers Karamazov*, II, p. 648.
17. *Existentialism and Humanism*, p. 34.
18. *The Quiet American*, p. 28.
19. *Ibid.*, p. 95. 20. *Ibid.*, p. 31. 21. *Ibid.*, p. 119.
22. *Ibid.*, p. 28. 23. *Ibid.*, p. 44. 24. *Ibid.*
25. *Ibid.*, p. 119. 26. *Ibid.*, p. 59. 27. *Ibid.*, p. 152.
28. *Ibid.*, p. 117. 29. *Ibid.*, p. 162. 30. *Ibid.*
31. *Ibid.*, p. 163. 32. *Ibid.*, p. 113.
33. Jean-Paul Sartre, *Iron in the Soul*, trans. Gerard Hopkins (London: Hamish Hamilton, 1950), Penguin Books, 1968, p. 61.
34. *The Quiet American*, p. 104.
35. Lawrence Lerner, "Love and Gossip: How Moral is Literature", *Essays in Criticism*, XIV (April 1964), 136.
36. *The Quiet American*, p. 167.
37. *Existentialism and Humanism*, p. 30.

38. *Being and Nothingness*, p. 598.
39. *The Quiet American*, p. 189.
40. David Lodge, *Graham Greene*, p. 36.
41. *The Quiet American*, p. 189.
42. *Mauvaise foi* translated as self-deception is one of the cardinal concepts in Sartrean existentialism. Unethical action is always characterized by that contradiction of the self by itself which he calls *Mauvaise foi*. *Existentialism and Humanism*, p. 16.
43. *The Quiet American*, p. 183.
44. J. Conrad, *Victory* (1915, London: Penguin Books, 1974), p. 40.
45. *Ibid.*, p. 87.
46. *The Quiet American*, p. 94.
47. *Ibid.*, p. 18. 48. *Ibid.*, p. 156. 49. *Ibid.*, p. 32.
50. *Ibid.*, p. 77. 51. *Ibid.* 52. *Ibid.*, p. 112.
53. *Ibid.*, p. 168. 54. *Ibid.*, p. 94.
55. Graham Greene, *The Comedians* (London: Bodley Head, 1966), Penguin Books, 1975, p. 43.
56. *Ibid.*, p. 175. 57. *Ibid.*, p. 111.
58. *Ibid.*, p. 130. 59. *Ibid.*
60. Walter Allen, *Tradition and Dream* (London: Phoenix House, 1964), Penguin Books, 1965, p. 223.
61. *The Comedians*, p. 25.
62. *Ibid.*, p. 198. 63. *Ibid.*, p. 263.
64. A. Camus, *The Fall*, trans. Justin O'Brien (London: Hamish Hamilton, 1957), Penguin Books, 1976, p. 66.
65. *The Comedians*, p. 196.
66. *Ibid.*, p. 236. 67. *Ibid.*, p. 255. 68. *Ibid.*, p. 281.
69. *Ibid.*, p. 236. 70. *Idid.*, p. 14.
71. *Ibid.*, p. 32. 72. *Ibid.*, p. 162.
73. *Nausea*, p. 216.
74. *The Comedians*, p. 279.
75. *Ibid.*, p. 161. 76. *Ibid.*, p. 235.
77. Fydor Dostoyevsky, *Notes From Underground*, trans. Jessie Coulson (London: Cox and Wyman, 1972), Penguin Books, 1977, p. 43.
78. *Ibid.*, p. 48.
79. *The Comedians*, p. 32.
80. *Ibid.*
81. *The End of the Affair*, p. 192.
82. David Lodge, *Graham Greene*, p. 44.

83. A. Camus, *The Myth of Sisyphus*, p. 21.
84. *Ibid.*, p. 53.
85. "Man seems to overcome the contradictions of his experience, its destructive or demonic element, by assuming the role of the anti-hero, the rebel-victim. The rebel denies without saying 'No' to life, the victim succumbs without saying 'Yes' to oppression." Ihab Hassan, *Radical Innocence: Studies in Contemporary American Novel* (Princeton: Princeton University Press, 1961), p. 31.
86. *The Comedians*, p. 266. 87. *Ibid.*
88. "The bastard is the individual who assumes our common and original bastardy, to do this of course, his particular situation must make it impossible for him to conceal that situation from himself as the rest of us are tempted to do." Francis Jeanson, "Hell and Bastardy", *Yale French Studies*, No. 30, p. 5.
89. *The Comedians*, p. 238.
90. *Ibid.*, p. 265. 91. *Ibid.*, p. 84. 92. *Ibid.*, p. 139.
93. *Ibid.*, p. 135. 94. *Ibid.*, p. 283. 95. *Ibid.*, p. 111.
96. *Ibid.*, p. 29. 97. *Ibid.*, p. 146.
98. *Ibid.*, p. 190. 99. *Ibid.*, p. 167. 100. *Ibid.*, p. 168.
101. *Ibid.*, p. 286. 102. *Ibid.*, p. 176. 103. *Ibid.*, p. 233.
104. "It's typical of Mexico of the whole human race perhaps—violence in favour of an ideal and then the ideal lost and the violence just going on." *The Lawless Roads*, p. 47.
105. *Ibid.*, p. 233. 106. *Ibid.*, p. 100.
107. Graham Greene, *The Honorary Consul* (London: Bodley Head, 1973), Penguin Books, 1974, p. 237.
108. *Ibid.*, p. 221. 109. *Ibid.*, p. 58. 110. *Ibid.*, p. 166.
111. *Ibid.*, p. 212. 112. *Ibid.*, p. 57. 113. *Ibid.*, p. 16.
114. *Ibid.*, p. 237. 115. *Ibid.*, p. 141. 116. *Ibid.*, p. 93.
117. *Ibid.*, p. 172. 118. *Ibid.*, p. 141. 119. *Ibid*, p. 142.
120. *Ibid.*, p. 81. 121. *Ibid.*, p. 267.
122. "Machismo—the sense of masculine pride—was the Spanish equivalent of *Virtus*." *The Honorary Consul*, p. 10.
123. *Ibid.*, p. 29. 124. *Ibid.*, p. 226. 125. *Ibid.*
126. *Ibid.*, p. 262. 127. *Ibid.*, p. 97. 128. *Ibid.*, p. 71.
129. *Ibid.*, p. 251. 130. *Ibid.*, p. 175. 131. *Ibid.*, p. 26.
132. *Ibid.*, p. 136. 133. *Ibid.* 134. *Ibid.*, p. 234.
135. *Ibid.*, pp. 211-12. 136. *Ibid.*

137. *Ibid.*, p. 171.
138. "Mine's a busy life, Leon, trying to cure the sick. I can't leave that to God." *The Honorary Consul*, p. 224.
139. *The Plague*, p. 126.
140. *The Honorary Consul*, p. 117.
141. *Ibid.*, p. 123. 142. *Ibid.*, p. 260. 143. *Ibid.*, p. 266.
144. Jean-Paul Sartre, *The Age of Reason*, trans. Eric Sutton (London: Hamish Hamilton, 1947), Penguin Books, 1970, p. 125.
145. *Ibid.*, p. 31. 146. *Ibid.*, p. 103. 147. *Ibid.*, p. 216.
148. *The Honorary Consul*, p. 219.
149. *Ibid.*, pp. 115-16. 150. *Ibid.*, p. 253.
151. *Ibid.*, p. 104. 152. *Ibid.*, p. 99.
153. "We define man only in relation to his commitments, it is therefore absurd to reproach us for irresponsibility in our choice . . . One chooses in view of others, and in view of others one chooses himself." *Existentialism and Humanism*, p. 50.
154. "The development of the feelings of ressentiment is the best evidence that self-awareness has been greatly diminished or destroyed and with it the power of choosing to be active in ways that are personally satisfying, expressive and effective in maintaining the rhythms of one's life in society." Lionel Rubinoff, "Liberty and the Contemporary Quest for Identity", *Queene's Quarterly*, No. 4, 85 (Winter 78-79), 569-70.
155. Graham Greene, *The Human Factor* (London: Bodley Head, 1978), Penguin Books, 1978, p. 20.
156. *Ibid.*, p. 141. 157. *Ibid.*, p. 32. 158. *Ibid.*, p. 120.
159. *Ibid.*, p. 22. 160. *Ibid.*, p. 166. 161. *Ibid.*, p. 115.
162. *Ibid.*, p. 184. 163. *Ibid.* 164. *Ibid.*, p. 208.
165. *Ibid.*, p. 125. 166. *Ibid.*, p. 33. 167. *Ibid.*, p. 87.
168. *Ibid.*, p. 212. 169. *Ibid.* 170. *Ibid.*
171. *Ibid.*, p. 81. 172. *Ibid.*, p. 87. 173. *Ibid.*, p. 129.
174. *Ibid.*, p. 48. 175. *Ibid.*, p. 128. 176. *Ibid.*, p. 129.
177. *Ibid.*, p. 189. 178. *Ibid.*, p. 190. 179. *Ibid.*, p. 122.
180. *Ibid.*, p. 201. 181. *Ibid.*, p. 96.
182. Uncle Remus is a code name for a secret plan of the USA, Great Britain, France and West Germany to aid South Africa in suppressing any revolution by black majority and to start a technological revolution. "It is purely a product of the author's imagination." Graham Greene's note to *The Human Factor*, p. 6.

183. *Ibid.*, p. 96. 184. *Ibid.*, p. 49. 185. *Ibid.*
186. *Ibid.*, p. 38. 187. *Ibid.*, p. 201. 188. *Ibid.*, p. 13.
189. *Ibid.*, p. 107. 190. *Ibid.*, p. 117. 191. *Ibid.*, p. 121.
192. *Ibid.*, p. 117. 193. *Ibid.*. p. 98. 194. *Ibid.*, p. 119.
195. *Ibid.*, p. 152. 196. *Ibid.*, p. 151.
197. J. Conrad, *Under Western Eyes* (J.M. Dent and Sons, 1911), Penguin Books, 1957, p. 262.
198. *Ibid.*, p. 278.
199. *The Human Factor*, p. 107.
200. *Ibid.*, p. 95. 201. *Ibid.*, p. 250. 202. *Ibid.*, p. 260.
203. *Ibid.*, p. 265.
204. *Existentialism and Humanism*, pp. 35-6.
205. *The Comedians*, p. 286.
206. *Ibid.*
207. F. Kafka, *The Trial* (London: Penguin Books, 1976), p. 134.
208. *Ibid.*, p. 135.
209. *The Comedians*, p. 286.

CHAPTER FOUR

Hints of a Vision: Short Stories

GRAHAM GREENE'S short stories written at long intervals between 1929 and 1963 portray the same world as his novels. One finds everywhere in these short stories the familiar Greene landscape and the familiar occupants who are lonely, bored and disgusted. The stories explore the same existential issues as the novels and contain more than a "hint of an explanation" towards the full understanding of Greene's existential vision.

The theme of death appears in some of his stories. A few years earlier he was preoccupied with death and even attempted to commit suicide. Now able to treat death existentially he seems to contend that death is a part of human condition. People usually fear death and want to postpone or transcend it. But "death will come in any case, and there is a long afterwards if the priests are right and nothing to fear if they are wrong."[1] Death is the final proof of the absurdity of both man and the universe. Greene seems to be as insistent as the existentialists on the need to face death as a reality. We can compare him with Heidegger who maintains that man can exist authentically only in the face of death. *Dasein* is a "being-towards-death". The being of the self comes to an end at death. The individual man dies and goes out of existence: "Death is the possibility of the absolute impossibility of *Dasein*."[2] Man is certain of his death but uncertain as to when it will occur. The constant threat of the possibility of death causes anxiety, in fact, it constitutes the experience of "care" in its extreme form. We are unable to escape death, but we can "will it".

"The End of the Party" (1929) is concerned with childhood fear and reminds us of Greene's "hatred"[3] for children's parties. Greene's later life and his literary production have been governed by fears experienced in childhood. While playing hide-and-seek in the dark, Francis Morton, a child of nervous disposition, whom his twin-brother Peter tries to protect and comfort, collapses to death at the unexpected touch of his brother. Conscious of the imminence of what he fears and his mind confused by a dozen contradictory plans, Francis stands alone in the dark planning to avoid the approaching terror of the dark. In the moments before his death, when he is in the mood of anxiety, he has an insight into the reality of his being. He becomes aware of the falsity of the reasoning of the grown-ups that "there's nothing to be afraid of in the dark",[4] for they themselves fearfully avoid the idea of it. Francis Morton's fear of darkness is a symbol of man's fear of death. He cries, "It will be a bad cold if I go to the party. Perhaps I shall die."[5] This is the existential anticipation of death. The anxiety or dread of death, "angst" as the existentialists call it, drives him into a tight corner, where he encounters death. Here we may call to mind Jones of *The Comedians* and Dr. Plarr of *The Honorary Consul*, who die accidentally. The story ends with Peter clutching his brother's dead fingers in puzzled grief: "His brain too young to realize the full paradox yet wondered with an obscure self-pity why it was that the pulse of his brother's fear went on and on, when Francis was now where he had always been told there was no more terror, no more darkness."[6] Francis Morton's fear of death going on and on even after he has collapsed, speaks of the significance of existence here and now. His death emphasizes the absurdity of man's life in which an individual's love and desire to help prove as destructive as hate. It points to the incomprehensibility of human life.

"The Second Death" (1929) is another story about death. Here a dying man is talking to his friend about his recovery from a previous illness and his encounter with God. The story insists on man's anxiety in the face of his death. The awful presence of death is embarrassing and frightening. The doctor, who thinks he is delirious, is no good to the dying man who wants "to be reassured".[7] The anticipation of death with definite certainty gives man a revelation of truth in his life, the pointlessness of the way he has lived. The moment before death is also the moment of self-knowledge. Though terrifying, "the taking of death with oneself" is also liberating. Death is a clue to authentic being. It frees us from servitude to petty cares that threaten to engulf our daily lives. The first line of one of the poems about death by Aquino of *The Honorary Consul* conveys this sense: "When death is on the tongue, the live man speaks."[8] This is the conclusion that seems to be echoed by Camus in *The Outsider*. The dying man in the story, like Andrews of *The Man Within*, acquires an authentic existence in the moments before death. He is awakened from the illusions of everyday life and tortures himself with the vision of hell: "There was someone there, all round me, who knew everything. Every girl I'd ever had. Even that young one who hadn't understood . . . Even the money I'd taken from mother. I never had a chance to explain."[9] We can compare the dying man with Jones of *The Comedians* who, playing at soldiers, understands the significance of confession in the face of death: "Death's a bloody serious affair. A man doesn't feel quite worthy of it. Like a decoration."[10] Like Jones, the dying man in the present story is full of remorse and feels the need of confession. He is released from the burden of his guilt when he makes confession to his friend. This reminds us of Camus speaking of the seriousness of death in *The Fall*: "Men are never convinced of your sincerity except by your death."[11]

Man is cast out into the world in order to die. Death is the capital possibility which devours all other possibilities. The caterpillar "dangling from the twig"[12] over a pool, whom the narrator is watching at the opening of the story, is suggestive of man's life in this world. The possibility of death is always present, yawning like a chasm, before man. But most men remain lost in the illusions of everyday life. They ignore the reality of death. The narrator cuts jokes to cheer up the dying man: "You needn't be frightened. You aren't going to die . . . You've got plenty more years in front of you, And plenty more girls too."[13] This is what Heidegger calls "evasive concealment in the face of death".[14] The narrator keeps talking the dying person into the belief that he will escape death and soon return to the tranquillized everydayness of the world of his concern. Such "solicitude" is meant to console him. In this manner he ("they" in Heidegger) provides a constant tranquillization about death. At bottom, however, this is a tranquillization not only for him who is dying but just as much for him who consoles him. But the narrator's tranquillity is upset at the actual sight of death. He is scared and wishes to "get away from his sly, bloodshot and terrified eyes and see something cheerful and amusing".[15] The narrator seeks to evade the implication of death by a process of self-deception.

The advance of medical science has helped man to live longer. It has greatly reduced the effects of senescence. Even death rate has fallen. But no one seriously believes that it can eliminate death. The doctor admits his weakness: ". . . he's going. There's nothing I can do."[16]

Thus the story shows the difference between the existential attitude of the man who lives in the face of the end and the man who systematically excludes the thought of death or seeks to do so. Greene's approach to the theme of death is existential. Like the existential thinkers, he speaks about one's anticipation of death and the anxiety it stirs. He is not concerned with the question of immortality but with the question of what the dread of death means for the human situation. He emphasizes the importance of life in this "world", it is authentic existence here and now which essentially is offered as a possibility for those who have accepted the finitude implied by death. Greene appears to be of the view, like Fortnum of *The Honorary Consul*, that there is no "afterwards".[17]

Despair, anxiety or "sickness unto death" is another important theme which has been emphatically treated in some of Greene's short stories. No longer the master of his own life, man has come under the possession of a number of mechanisms beyond his understanding and control and suffers from a sense of powerlessness, abandonment and indifference. He is angst-ridden and has neither desire nor zest for life. "A chance for Mr. Lever" and "A Drive in the Country" very well illustrate this theme.

"A Chance for Mr. Lever" (1936) describes Mr. Lever's despairing trip through the dangerous Liberian forest to find out a man named Davidson with whose help he hopes to make his fortune. An old man, retired from business ten years ago, he is gripped with a deep sense of disappointment that he has "to go from door to door asking for a job"[18] in his old age. In agreement with the plan of Mr. Lucas, the owner of a small engineering firm, he sets out on his arduous adventure, "a journey without map". He is full of doubt that he will ever find Davidson, his men refuse to cooperate with him and he is scared of "being deserted, scared of being made to return".[19] On his way he has to put up in thatched huts with "cockroaches the size of black-beetles flattened against the mud wall"[20] and the rats "rushing down the walls like water".[21] He feels sick and tired and is seized with the feeling of nausea. He thinks that he is "too old for this country".[22] He meets Davidson who is in a state of unconsciousness and whose body is covered with blood and black vomit. He finds only death, squalor and no return. He is flared into rebellion and rejects old cliches and recognizes "nothing but one personal relationship, his affection for Emily",[23] *i.e.*, his wife. This is in agreement with Greene's usual outlook. In his fiction he has exposed the hollowness of conventional morality. But the love of someone or the other always remains sound: Kate's in *England Made Me*, Rose's in *Brighton Rock*, Scobie's in *The Heart of the Matter*, Bandrix's in *The End of the Affair*.

The story stresses on the contingent nature of man's life. Man must give in to contingency. Mr. Lever, like Sartre's hero Mathiew, allows himself to sink. Though facing the hurdles of life, he is allowed only three days of happiness while returning with "his amateurish forgeries and the infection of yellow fever in the blood".[24] This points to the sense of "the absurd"[25] in life, the discrepancy between man's desire for happiness and the hostile and indifferent universe.

"A Drive in the Country" (1937) is a story with a socio-economic background. The central character is Fred, a young man, a victim of unemployment, for whom suicide is the only way out. The story embodies the theme of anxiety and hopelessness man is suffering from in the modern busy urban life and points out that both possession and deprivation have dehumanizing effect on man. The girl who is in love with Fred feels terribly bored in her parents' house. Her father, a head clerk in Bergson's Export Agency, is a dehumanized figure: "His home was like his office, run on the same lines, its safety preserved with the same meticulous care, so that he could present a faithful steward's account to the managing director."[26] Like Krogh, the rich man of *England Made Me*, he is always preoccupied with the enhancement of his property. After a good meal he is in the habit of saying: "I've improved the property . . . I've wired this room for power, . . . this radiator', the final stroke of satisfaction, the garden."[27]

But he pays a heavy price for his sense of property. His possession of wealth deprives him of his humanity. His own daughter is full of contempt for him. She tries to escape the boredom of her home through her love for a young man. Fred, on the other hand, is in a state of deprivation. Fred's misery is his unemployment in spite of all his efforts he has failed to get himself employed. He is full of resentment against life, which is almost a hell: "It's the hell of a life."[28] He has a sense of total helplessness and, like Pinkie in *Brighton Rock*, suggests to his girl a suicide pact to which the girl does not agree. Pleading for life, she insists on finding out "some way. . ."[29] to go on living. But Fred, who has lost all hope for a job, reflects: "It's no good hoping that I'll get a job . . . There aren't any more jobs any more. And every year . . . there's less chance."[30] In a state of hopelessness he kills himself and the girl comes back to her parent's house to suffer the worst boredom of life.

Thus Greene's theme in "A Chance for Mr. Lever" and "A Drive in the Country" is despair. The impotence of individual effort and discontent induce a feeling of despair. Despair and hope are correlated in respect of Mr. Lever. Mr. Lever trusts in the future. In the case of Fred, despair leads to suicide and Mr. Lever dies of yellow fever. The contrary of suicide, in fact, is man condemned to death. One is reminded of Marcel who deals with despair at length in his *Being and Having*. He is a critic of present-day materialistic society. He looks upon "having" as a source of alienation. Those who "have" are in a state of tension and those who have not suffer from a sense of resentment. The world is so constructed that absolute despair appears inevitable in it: "Despair is, so to speak, the shock felt by the mind when it meets with 'there is no more'."[31]

"The Basement Room" (1936) is one of Greene's best stories. In it Philip, a small boy, is left by his parents in the care of the butler and his wife. He sees his friend, the butler, commit murder. The two worlds in the story which Philip must recognize and choose between are separated by a green baize door. Philip is required to make a "journey without map".

The details of the house and the reference to nurses and the presence of the servants indicate that Philip, like Greene himself, has been brought up in fairly comfortable circumstances. But he suffers from estrangement and loneliness in his own house. He feels alienated from his parents and he is at ease when they are away. The servants are loveless and perform their duty for their livelihood. Philip feels "a stranger in his home because he could go into any room and all the rooms" are "empty".[32]

Philip dreams of autonomy, of free will, though his internal resources are too feeble: "He felt very old, independent and judicial, he was aware that Baines was talking to him as man to man."[33] But a child's capacity for freedom is smaller than an adult's. A child is not capable of self-discipline like an adult. Philip feels anger and disappointment when he is tricked into telling Baines's secret: ". . .the responsibility for Baines weighing on his spirit".[34] The idea of keeping Mrs. Baines's secret when he has failed to keep Mr. Baines's makes him "miserable with the unfairness of life."[35] He suffers from a bitter sense of anxiety in the adult world which is incomprehensible to him. The anxiety arises from a distrust of himself and his reactions. The things he does not understand terrify him: "the basement held its secrets, the green baize door shut off that world."[36] His innocent mind is gripped with a sense of unfairness and utter unreason of life: "The sensation of disappointment was one which Philip could share; knowing nothing of love or jealousy or passion he could understand better than anyone this grief, something hoped for not happening, something promised not fulfilled, something exciting turning dull."[37] Philip is, therefore, unwilling to get involved in the world of Mr. and Mrs. Baines. He firmly decides to keep himself away from the world he is unable to understand: "Let grown-up people keep to their world and he would keep to his, safe in the small garden between the plane-trees."[38]

But the walls separating the two worlds are torn down and he is drawn into the grown-up world without willing it in the manner Mathieu of Sartre's *Roads to Freedom* is drawn into the vortex of war. Philip's involvement, like that of Sartre's hero, arises partly from his own moral constitution and partly from the environment from which he cannot withdraw. The sight of the housekeeper's crumpled body drags him into the horrifying world. After the murder he runs away from the house in utter disgust and returns to the house in the policeman's company. The event leaves its mark on the whole of his later development. Thus life falls upon him with all its savagery. He is frightened and dies "the old dilettante, sixty years later with nothing to show rather than preserve the memory of Mrs. Baines's malicious voice".[39]

Philip bears the same relation to the grown-up life beyond him as a man to the vast world. Man, like the child, can neither reach and understand himself nor grasp the unreasonable, illogical and absurd world. As he tries to relate himself to the world around him, he loses contact not only with that world but also with himself. The story conveys the modern sense of ontological lostness and bewilderment set forth in Franz Kafka's *The Castle*, as we read of the surveyor's unavailing attempts to get into touch with the real forces that determine his life.

Greene, like Sartre, lays stress on the freedom and responsibility of the individual. To Sartre, ". . .the reason for our acts is in ourselves. We act as we are. Our acts contribute to making us."[40] Man's freedom is limited by facticity and possibility. On one side, man is free and projects his possibilities, on the other side, he is constricted by the factual situation. However, man is the master of his destiny and he is free, free in everyway, free to behave like a fool, or a machine, free to accept, free to refuse, free to equivocate. He can do what he likes. There is for him no good nor evil unless he brings them into being. All around him things are gathered in a circle expectant, impassive and indicative of nothing. He is alone, enveloped in the monstrous silence, free and alone without assistance and without excuse, condemned to decide without support from any quarter. Greene is acquainted with the liberal progressive outlook prevailing in our time and points out that Philip, like Pinkie, is what his indifferent parents have made him. Philip's all genuine willing has been paralysed and a genuine future and genuine possibilities have been cut off by a massive awareness of what has been. He, however, as Greene suggests, is not fully determined by his environment. He is always aware of his freedom and responsibility and is ultimately responsible for what he becomes because he is always free to behave otherwise. The story lays stress on the freedom of the individual and the contingent nature of life. Even in childhood, though the scope for freedom is comparatively limited, the individual is free to forge his destiny. Trying to preserve his personal freedom, the individual gets involved with others, as does Philip in the present story, because the universe and man's own existence are too complex to be grasped by human intelligence.

Many of Greene's stories, which appeared in the later phase of his literary career, are concerned with the problem of faith. Faith is vital and indescribable. He, who has it, knows what it is, and perhaps also he who sincerely and painfully knows, he is without it, has some inkling of what it is. Faith cannot be described to a thoroughly rational mind. Faith partakes of the mystery of life itself.

"The Hint of an Explanation" (1948) conveys by means of a parable the mysterious nature of faith. A priest relates to a fellow-traveller how oddly he caught a glimpse of his faith in his childhood. As a child he attended Mass and participated in church service. But he was full of disgust for the formalities of the church. He was afraid of losing his place in the service and doing something ridiculous. He says: "Every Sunday I had to dress up in my surplice and serve Mass. I hated it—I have always hated dressing up in any way."[41] Religious service was no aid to his faith. It is the horrible and ingenious plan of Blacker, a free thinker and a well-known baker in the village, to corrupt the boy probably to avenge himself on the Catholics and also to soothe his personal grudge against the boy's father, a bank manager, for some unsatisfactory dealing in the bank, offers the boy the glimpses of faith. The fear of death and the longing to possess the electric train drive the boy to carry out Blacker's instructions to give him a wafer for communion. But in the last moment, Blacker's plan to corrupt the boy is defeated. The boy, who is shocked and stunned, suddenly feels the presence of God in the form of the Host in the room. He gets the first hints of his faith in the baker's inexplicable anxious longing for the wafer which is "only a bit of bread"[42] to an unbeliever. He anticipates Sarah of *The End of the Affair* whose faith is confirmed by the rationalist preacher Richard Smythe's arguments against the existence of God.

Greene in this story insists on the paradoxical nature of faith. A man endowed with intuition may be surprised into believing in the existence of God. But when he comes across senseless suffering in the world, he, like the agnostic traveller in the present story, revolts at the notion of a God who abandons his creatures to the enormities of free will. The agnostic traveller says: "When you think what God—if there is a God—allows. It's not merely the physical agonies, but think of the corruption even of children. . . ."[43] One is reminded of Dr. Colin of *A Burnt-out Case* who does not "care to believe in him"[44] (God) who allows even a three-year-old child suffer from leprosy and Dr. Rieux who refuses to "love a scheme of things in which children are put to torture."[45] The story stresses that God is a mystery and He surpasses succinct explanation. One can catch signs and sometimes they are too faint to be grasped by man's intelligence. Clarifying the doubts of the agnostic fellow-passenger, David remarks: "We catch hints. . .And they mean nothing at all to another human being than the man who catches them. They are not scientific evidence—or evidence at all for that matter."[46] The journey here becomes a symbol of life. The train passes through many dark tunnels and leaves the travellers in complete darkness. The light is poor and strains their eyesight. Man's intelligence is that half-light making our view so limited, but it is the only light with which one can catch hints of so many inexplicable things. The frequent light failures symbolize the dull grey days of our lives when we are at a loss to cope with the mystery of life. Man, who seeks a rational explanation of all things, fails to reach faith. Faith absolutely contradicts reason. Faith illumines man in moments of despair and anxiety.

"A Visit to Morin" (1957) is another story concerned with the problem of faith. Here Greene points out the inadequacy of "the scholastic arguments for the existence of God".[47] Mr. Morin is "an old French novelist once famous but now disgruntled and half-forgotten."[48] He can be easily identified with Greene. He hits out vigorously at his fellow Catholics. He "had offended the orthodox Catholics in his own country and pleased the liberal Catholics abroad. . .he used to find enthusiastic readers among non-Christians who. . .perhaps detected in his work the freedom of speculation which put his fellow-Catholics on their guard."[49] His conversation with the narrator, an Englishman, Mr. Dunlop, who has been reading his works since the age of sixteen, reveals Greene's outlook on faith. Mr. Morin says that one must avoid theology if one wants to believe. He doubts the capacity of the human mind. He says, "A man can accept anything to do with God until scholars begin to go into the details and the implications. A man can accept the Trinity, but the arguments that follow. . . ."[50] It is an astonishing thing about Morin that he has been separated from the church for twenty years and that he is afraid to go back: "If I went back and belief did not return? That is what I fear, Mr. Dunlop. As long as I keep away from the sacraments, my lack of belief is an argument for the church. But if I returned and they failed me then I would really be a man without faith . . . ."[51]

Here Greene seems to be of the view that faith is trust before it is belief. Belief is the articles, creeds and tenets of a church. Faith as a concrete mode of being of the human person precedes faith as the intellectual assent to a proposition. Faith is a paradox. It is not reached by arguments nor can one acquire faith by following the rules of the church. Mr. Morin, like the Priest, Rose, Scobie and Sarah, acquires faith without following the rituals of the church. Greene, like Christian existentialists, emphasizes faith springing from man's within and points out the irrelevance of the formalities of an organized religion. His works show the significance of faith based on man's free will.

"Under the Garden" (1963) is a small masterpiece concerning the sense of reality. There are two parts of reality for man—one is accessible, intelligible and manageable and the other is its opposite. The accessible part is just a fragment of the whole. It does not make a coherent sense. The key to a full understanding of reality lies in the other inaccessible part. Greene, like Kierkegaard, seems close to adopting an irrationalism. To Greene, as to Kierkegaard, reality goes beyond reason. In the present story a man named Wilditch, learning that he has lung cancer and must have a major operation, is disappointed at the abruptness with which he is thrust off the conveyor-belt "into the world of choice again".[52] Unwilling to "appear dialectical"[53] and having "no curiosity at all about the future",[54] he goes to stay at the house where he passed much of his childhood. He is haunted by a dream from his childhood about a lake with an island in it. The lake actually is a pond in which, as his brother says, "the water's nowhere more than two feet deep".[55] The dream seems so vivid that he cannot feel quite certain that it is a dream at all. He re-reads the story written in his childhood for a school magazine, a conventional story about a buried treasure and comes across the rude remarks of his mother on the margin. He recollects his mother, a Fabian socialist, who could not understand that the tale was a good intellectual exercise for a boy of thirteen. She apprehended that the boy was "subjected" to some "religious instructions".[56] She had very decided views about any mystery and wanted everything to be very clear and did not approve of fairy stories. Her extreme views subdued Wilditch's imaginative power. Wilditch's mother, like the mother of James Callifer in *The Potting Shed*, appears to be modelled on Greene's own mother who was unable to understand children's taste for wonder. Like Greene, Wilditch was bored and stayed away from home for hours so as to dispel his boredom. His struggle against boredom went on throughout his life. The gardener reflects: "... he hasn't changed, he's off hunting for something, like he always did, though I doubt if he knows what he's after."[57] Even in his later life, there was no scope for the full play of his imagination. In various services he was employed, he was required to supply facts, "imagination was usually a quality to be suppressed .... Speculation was discouraged."[58] Wilditch, therefore, has been all his life a wanderer and an outcast: "A restless man, never long in one place, no wife, no children".[59] He has suffered from anguish springing from an abundance of unrealized power and loss of identity.

The story emphatically deals with the theme of boredom. In

insisting on the effect of boredom on man's life, Greene seems to be coming close to Marcel, to whom boredom is the most dangerous thing "for spiritual development".[60] The feeling of boredom upsets the spiritual development of Wilditch. His dream of the "tunnel" and the "bearded man" and the "hidden treasure" though not recognized by his rationalist mother has been more than just a dream seen during the course of a night's truancy. It stayed with him throughout his life and made him restless. All his life he has been concerned to identify it with the actual life experience. He says: "... of course it had all been a dream, ... but a dream too was an experience."[61] Wilditch's dream points to the presence of the irrational and mysterious elements in life. A dream, as the modern psychologists suggest, can only contain what one has experienced or if we have sufficient faith in Jung, what our ancestors have experienced. But Wilditch dreams about "calor-gas" and "beauty contests" which are not "ancestral memories nor the memories of a child of seven."[62] His dream certifies the incomprehensible nature of the human mind and the child's natural inclination towards the irrational and inexplicable. The irrational, as it happens in the case of Wilditch, plays a very significant role in man's life. Greene insists on the need of accepting the irrational. He seems to be of the view that life is diminished by too narrow a rationalism. He points out that the rich strands of human existence should not be ignored only because they cannot be fitted into logic.

"Dream of a Strange Land" (1963) also raises the same issues of reality and unreality as "Under the Garden". Herr Professor, a distinguished retired doctor, refuses to attend upon a leper as it is against law. He, however, violates the law when he allows a second visitor, a Colonel, to celebrate the General's birthday in his house. The celebration is carried out and the doctor feels lost in his own home.

The doctor is an enlightened man, having a large number of books on medical science in his study, a heavy desk bearing a bronze paperweight representing "Prometheus chained to his rock with a hovering eagle thrusting its beak into his liver".[63] His study and profession have dehumanized him so much that he only understands his legal duty and the things he has read in books. His loyalty to accepted opinions deprives him of his subjectivity. He fails to set aside the rules and exercise his existential freedom. He feels no pity for the leper helplessly imploring him not to refer him to a hospital as it will ruin him. He blindly sticks to the law: "contagious cases must always go to the hospital."[64] He is unable to understand that "leprosy is a word—it's not a disease".[65] Leprosy can be cured but no one can cure a word. It is incomprehensible to the doctor that even if leprosy is stripped of all its stigma, a leprosy patient develops complexes arising out of disfigurement. Thus the doctor stands in contrast to Dr. Colin of *A Burnt-out Case*, who has sympathy for the patients and who understands that "...for the burnt-out cases life outside isn't easy. They carry the stigma of leprosy. People are apt to think once a leper, always a leper."[66]

The doctor feels "far from home as though he were living in a strange country"[67] during the celebration of the General's birthday with music, dance, drinking and gambling. He tries to soothe himself reading Scopenhauer. The patient too finds himself in a wrong country when he comes back to the doctor's house, "ablaze with light and noisy with voices"[68] in the midst of the party. He is bewildered as there is "no Prometheus, no doctor even to whom he could appeal".[69] Now his home seems to be "too far away".[70] In utter despair he kills himself with a revolver. The self-assured doctor is horrified at the faint explosion and his sense of reality is shaken.

Through the characters of the doctor and the leper, Greene insists on the modern man's intense feeling of homelessness and alienation in the midst of a bureaucratized impersonal society. He points out that truth is not what one knows merely by intellect but what one knows with one's whole being. A slave to system, man is unable to feel and respond in sincerity to his real self. The rule-bound conduct ruins man's capacity to behave naturally and spontaneously.

Some other stories too deal with existential themes. The theme of "I Spy" (1930) is self-alienation. Like Andrews of *The Man Within*, Charlie Stowe, a boy of twelve, is alienated from his own self as well as from his parents. Like Andrews, he is anxious to assert his real self. "Proof Positive" (1930) raises the question of body-soul relationship and suggests that the spirit outlives the body and tastes eternity; but without the body's aid the spirit decays into "whispered nonsense".[71] The story stresses the significance of the body, the concrete existence here and now, and thus reverses the traditional concept in which the soul is significant and the body does not matter. Greene's stance with regard to the body and the soul seems to be in agreement with Sartre's views on the "in-itself" and the "for-itself", the body and the consciousness: ". . . the for-itself without the in-itself is a kind of abstraction, it could not exist any more than a color could exist without form or a sound without pitch and without timbre."[72]

"A Day Saved" (1935) conveys a sense of life's meaninglessness. One can't live indefinitely. Death is inevitable and so there is no point in saving a day. "Brother" (1936) offers a criticism of Communism which is unduly *a priori* and unduly dogmatic. Like Sartre, Greene insists on the notion of free individual men. "The Innocent" (1937) is concerned with man's awareness of an inner void. He is conscious of his inability to feel as intensely as he did in his childhood. Visiting the place of his birth and early education in the company of his girl, the narrator feels fascinated towards the place. "It is the smell of innocence"[73] that holds him. The obscene picture drawn in his boyhood reminds him of his passionate love for a girl. He is filled with remorse and longs for "the purity, the intensity, the pain of that passion".[74] "Across the Bridge" (1938) and "The Case for the Defence" (1939) are concerned with man's baseless optimism that is much more appalling than despair. In "Across the Bridge", Joseph Calloway, a proud millionaire, magnified by colossal theft and world-wide pursuit, escapes arrest but he is run over by a car and dies "in a mess of broken glass and gold rims and silver hair and blood. The dog . . . licking and whimpering and licking."[75] In "The Case for the Defence", a murderer, in spite of a water-tight case and four eye-witnesses, escapes conviction and while coming out of the court crowded with people, is fatally knocked down by a truck. These two stories insist on man's dehumanization in the present-day urban society and ironically point out the inefficiency of human law. In "Men at Work" (1940), Richard Skate, a civil servant in the Establishment branch of the Ministry of Propaganda, a thin, pale, hungry-looking man in his early middle age, is cut off from his wife and child and visits them hurriedly only twice a week. He represents the modern man lost in the superficial glamour of life and engaged in futile work. "Propaganda was a means of passing the time: work was not done for its usefulness but for its own sake—simply as an occupation."[76] The mythical symbol of mankind is Sisyphus, the ancient hero who was condemned to spend his days rolling a boulder to the top of a hill, always to see it escape him and crash back down to the bottom.

This brief analysis of some of his important stories reveals the presence of existential issues that dominate Greene's novels. The important existential themes projected in these stories are freedom, decision and responsibility as also guilt, alienation, despair and death.

Notes and References

1. *The Honorary Consul*, p. 123.
2. Heidegger, *Being and Time*, p. 214.
3. "I hated the very idea of children's parties." *A Sort of Life*, p. 25.
4. Graham Greene, *Twenty-one Short Stories* (London: William Heinemann, 1954), Penguin Books, 1970, p. 38.
5. *Ibid.*, p. 35.
6. *Ibid.*, p. 43.
7. *Ibid.*, p. 125.
8. *The Honorary Consul*, p. 123.
9. *Twenty-one Short Stories*, pp. 125-26.
10. *The Comedians*, p. 263.
11. *The Fall*, pp. 55-6.
12. *Twenty-one Short Stories*, p. 122.
13. *Ibid.*, p. 125.
14. *Being and Time*, p. 298.
15. *Twenty-one Short Stories*, p. 126.
16. *Ibid.*, p. 124.
17. "I don't know anything about that 'afterwards'. I only know I would like to live another ten years, at my camp, watching the little bastard grow." *The Honorary Consul*, p. 123.
18. *Twenty-one Short Stories*, p. 97.
19. *Ibid.*, p. 102.
20. *Ibid.*, p. 94.
21. *Ibid.*, p. 102.
22. *Ibid.*, p. 101.
23. *Ibid.*, p. 107.
24. *Ibid.*, p. 109.
25. "The absurd is the contrary of hope...", *The Myth of Sisyphus*, p. 37.
26. *Twenty-one Short Stories*, p. 52.
27. *Ibid.*, p. 53.
28. *Ibid.*, p. 55.
29. *Ibid.*, p. 60.
30. *Ibid.*, p. 59.
31. *Being and Having*, p. 102.
32. *Twenty-one Short Stories*, p. 7.
33. *Ibid.*, p. 9.
34. *Ibid.*, p. 17.
35. *Ibid.*
36. *Ibid.*, p. 16.
37. *Ibid.*, pp. 10-1.
38. *Ibid.*, p. 25.
39. *Ibid.*, p. 17.
40. Sartre, *Being and Nothingness*, p. 583.
41. *Twenty-one Short Stories*, p. 113.

42. *Ibid.*, p. 120. 43. *Ibid.*, p. 111.
44. *A Burnt-out Case*, p. 199.
45. *The Plague*, p. 203.
46. *Twenty-one Short Stories*, p. 112.
47. Graham Greene, *A Sense of Reality* (London: Bodley Head, 1963), Penguin Books, 1972, p, 75.
48. Atkins, *Graham Greene*, p. 212.
49. *A Sense of Reality*, p. 65.
50. *Ibid.*, p. 74. 51. *Ibid.*, p. 78. 52. *Ibid.*, p. 11.
53. *Ibid.*, p. 13. 54. *Ibid.* 55. *Ibid.*, p. 18.
56. *Ibid.*, p. 22. 57. *Ibid.*, p. 61. 58. *Ibid.*, p. 16.
59. *Ibid.*, p. 14.
60. *Metaphysical Journal*, p. 236.
61. *A Sense of Reality*, p. 24.
62. *Ibid.*, p. 42. 63. *Ibid.*, p. 80.
64. *Ibid.*, p. 81. 65. *Ibid.*, p. 82.
66. *A Burnt-out Case*, p. 123.
67. *A Sense of Reality*, p. 88.
68. *Ibid.*, p. 90. 69. *Ibid.*, p.92. 70. *Ibid.*, p. 91.
71. *Twenty-one Short Stories*, p. 93.
72. *Being and Nothingness*, p. 790.
73. *Twenty-one Short Stories*, p. 48.
74. *Ibid.*, p. 51. 75. *Ibid.*, p. 75. 76. *Ibid.*, p. 161.

CHAPTER FIVE

Hints of a Vision: Plays

GRAHAM GREENE is a novelist who believes, "one must try every drink once".[1] Though he had "attempted the theatre"[2] around 1920, his successful plays were written in the second phase of his literary career when he was engaged in a restless search for new themes and new modes of exploring them. A master of his craft, he liked unity, and the severities of a firm pattern were stimulating to him. He wanted to write not "a producer's play" but "an author's play".[3] Like all major artists, Greene created in these plays a world informed by his own outlook and vision. In them too, as we shall see, important existential issues are effectively treated.

The Living Room is the first successful play of Greene. The plot centres round Rose, the daughter of a Catholic mother and a non-Catholic father. Lately orphaned, she begins a love-affair with a middle-aged psychologist, her trustee, on the night of her mother's funeral. She comes to stay with her two old aunts of her uncle, a crippled priest. They live in a large London house, yet in cramped conditions. All the bedrooms in which some or the other has died are closed, and now they have just the "living room". The aunts and the uncle are shown as being misguided and uncomprehending and they oppose and frustrate the lovers' desire for happiness. Rose finds herself caught up between the pain of giving up her lover and the pain of hurting his wife. The conflict leads in the end to a despair akin to Scobie's and she takes her own life.

The elderly foolish Catholic women, who are drawn critically, are the orthodox members of the church. They do not understand the essentials of their own religion. Helen is the narrower and more bigoted of the two. The unhappy victims of the fear of death, they don't like using a room in which somebody has ever died. Their silly fear of death is a sign of their lack of faith in God. No one who believes in God should fear death. Their brother James remarks: "Perhaps it's the fear of death—of the certainty of death. They don't seriously mind accidents . . . It's the inevitable they hate . . . In mercy. My sisters don't seem to have any trust."[4] These women are good Catholics, they are never wicked nor are they impelled by evil motives. They have holy books and holy pictures and perform religious rites. They sincerely believe that they are right in all their actions. But actually they are incomplete and stupid and they do not understand what is right. Their lack of charity precipitates the tragedy. When Rose comes to stay with them, they do not understand her situation. They watch her movements and wish to stop her affair with the psychologist. It is their unsympathetic attitude, probably the outcome of their religious piety, that drives Rose to suicide. James observes: "We've ruined her between us . . . Don't blame him. Blame our dead goodness. Holy books, holy pictures, a subscription to the Altar Society."[5]

The champion of the church, of course, is James, an invalid priest. He lost his one leg in an automobile accident twenty years ago. His physical handicap is the symbol of the helplessness of the church. He understands that his sisters' idea of shutting up the bedrooms is ridiculous and unreasonable. They do it because of their pervasive fear of the inevitable. But he has no courage to protest until Rose dies. He has unwillingly allowed the foolishness about the rooms to go on. He regrets not to have fought with his sisters to stop them from closing the rooms: "It was wrong of me to give way about those rooms. When it began it seemed silly and unimportant."[6] He makes broad-minded remarks and appears to be very anxious to help human beings in distress: "I dream of helping somebody in great trouble. Saying the right word at the right time."[7]

He is given the chance, as Rose comes to him for help. But the priest fails in his duty. He strives for the right word but can find none except formulas. He is anxious to be of use but his "tongue is heavy with the Penny Catechism".[8] Here one calls to mind the old priest of *Brighton Rock* who talks of "the appalling strangeness of the mercy of God" and Father Rank, the priest of *The Heart of the Matter*, who says, "The church knows all the rules" when faced with the human problem. Father James can say nothing except: "Dear, there's always the Mass. It's there to help. Your Rosary, you've got a Rosary . . . Perhaps Our Lady . . . prayer."[9] The play is full of spiritual snobbery. All the characters are conscious of their self-importance. The priest's spiritual pride is roused when the psychologist, Mr Michael, uses a jargon. The way the priest sneers at

Mr. Michael is probably the most unpleasant feature of the play: "You can't fob off a Catholic with a registrar's signature and call it a marriage."[10]

The way these old people treat Rose is suggestive of their lack of sympathetic understanding. Rose feels lost in the wood of old people. Passionately in love with Mr. Michael and in full awareness of what she is doing, she is determined to go away with him. Her love is similar to Rose's love for Pinkie in that it is not childish infatuation which can disppear when faced with hurdles. The thought of the church and illegitimate children cannot shake her:

"Michael: My plans haven't been a success. My wife won't divorce me. We may never be able to marry.

Rose: . . . It doesn't really matter, does it? It wouldn't have been a real marriage . . .

Michael: You don't mind—about the church.

Rose: Oh, I expect it will come all right in the end. I shall make a death-bed confession and die in the odour of sanctity.

Michael: Our children will be illegitimate.

Rose: Bastards are the best . . . ."[11]

Rose's affair is something illicit and outrageous to the aunts. It's a mortal sin to them. All including the priest oppose it and insist on their separation. But for this sacrifice they have to offer only fear and pious platitudes which fill Rose with bitter contempt. It's really awful. She remarks: " . . . I can't bear this house. It gives me the creeps."[12] The conflict between her desire for happiness and the opposition from the representatives of the church is movingly presented. Helen claims to have kept her in the church and thinks that Rose will go to the confession. Rose, on the other hand, has no love for the church and its constricting rules. They stir a feeling of revulsion in Rose. She ridicules Helen's thought of confession: "And do it again, and go to confession, and do it again? Do you call that better than having children, living together till we die?"[13]

She is more concerned with life here in this world, formulas do not fascinate her. She only wants a bit of ordinary human comfort. She can "live a life-time without the sacraments. That wouldn't hurt—but a life-time, without him . . . ."[14] In the meanwhile, Mrs. Michael appears on the scene. The pathetic sight of the hysteric woman with her husband is unbearable to Rose. Her mind is now in torment. After having seen the man with his wife, it is not possible for her to go ahead with her plan. She is torn by a conflict between the burden of bearing another's existence and her own suffering without love. She is distressed and puzzled at the sight of them together: "I can't think about people I don't know. She was just a name, that's all. And then she comes here and beats her fists on the table and cries in the chair. I saw them together. They are married . . . Oh, he told me they were, but I hadn't seen them . . . It was just like something in a book, but now I have seen them together . . . Tell me what to do, Father."[15] She is now angst-ridden. The horror of her own life with her aunts in an atmosphere of constant fear and the horror of inflicting suffering on another woman shake her terribly. In utter helplessness she turns to her uncle and urges him to give her peace. But the priest can only ask her to pray to God which only rouses her hatred for Him: "Don't talk to me about God or the saints. I don't believe in your God who took away your legs and wants to take away Michael. I don't believe in your church and Holy Mother of God. I don't believe. I don't believe."[16] Rose, like Scobie, dislikes God who allows suffering in this world. The notion of God as an enemy is a recurring theme in Greene. One is reminded of Bendrix who thinks God as his rival. He says: "You're a devil, God, tempting us to leap . . . With your great schemes you ruin our happiness."[17] All human help is denied to her. She does not care for divine mercy. Her dilemma is insoluble. Like Scobie, she cannot seek absolution for an act she intends to commit again. The future appears to her completed before it is even lived. She cannot outlive the tension created in her by the conflict between her love and horror. Consequently she succumbs to despair. There is nothing she can do except withdrawing herself from the world. She commits suicide, an unpardonable sin for a Catholic and is now a "stone in a pond".[18] But her death becomes the channel of other's salvation. The elder and the weaker of the sisters enters carrying a load of bedding. She is firmly determined to sleep in the room where Rose died. The other sister, panic-stricken, tries to prevent her, but their brother at last asserts his authority. She collapses across the bed crying like a child. Her hard heart is broken now.

The Living Room develops the theme of despair in relation to an impossible physical love. The pressure of existence becomes so unbearable that Rose breaks down from sheer impotence and self-destruction remains the only way of resolving the difficulties. Man, like Rose, is "thrown" into the world, he is abandoned in it. The impotence of the individual effort in the vast scheme of the universe induces despair. Despair, Gabriel Marcel says, is an expression of "the will to 'negation' as applied to being".[19] Man despairs of discovering the utter unreason of a completely broken world. It was on the grounds that Greene reduced hope in his books "to its least denominator"[20] that Gabriel Marcel, who was known as the Catholic existentialist, did claim Greene as one of them.

A devastating criticism of the church is implied by the characters of the play. Greene's clerical outlook offends Catholic readers who think that "their supposed apologist was really subversive".[21] Greene refers to it in his autobiography, "Catholics have sometimes accused me of making my clerical characters, Father Rank in *The Heart of the Matter* and Father James in *The Living Room,* fail unnecessarily before the human problems they were made to face."[22] He is of the view that the priest should be capable of a deeper comprehension of human problems. Father Talbot, who had great human sympathy, had no solution for Greene's problem. He could help Greene in the critical moment of his life telling him to follow his conscience which even then was elastic enough for almost anything. Greene defends the individual against dogma and shows the significance of the love of God and the love for a corrupt and suffering humanity.

Greene's criticism of the conventional piety and the rules of the church and its insistence on the insignificance of human lot in this world links him to Kierkegaard, the Christian existentialist. Kierkegaard is angry with institutionalized Christianity for it devalues the worth of human personality, and destroys the individuality of man and also his power of decision-making. Like Kierkegaard, Greene is hard on the agents of the Catholic church who are incapable of coping with human crisis. Their preoccupation with the other forms of religion takes over and pushes out the essential belief, compassion, mercy, forgiveness, trust and love. Thus *The Living Room,* like Greene's religious novels, emphasizes the theme of despair, "sickness unto death" and the irrelevance of conventional piety and the rules of the church which deprive man of his existential freedom. It insists on the significance of human love and suffering.

The Potting Shed is Greene's second work for the theatre. The playwright's main concern in this play is to establish the force of the supernatural. Scientific rationalism, which is characteristic of the present century, insists on a reasonable explanation of everything. But there are things in life which are beyond the grasp of human intelligence. As they are inexplicable, they appear meaningless to the rationalist mind. Graham Greene insists on the significance of the mysterious elements of life and pleads for their acceptance. He suggests that rationalism represents only a small segment of the whole and concrete man, and it must accord recognition to the mysterious and the irrational.

The Potting Shed is an attempt to draw "a hollow man". He makes a better attempt in *A Burnt-out Case*. James Callifer, who is engaged in the task of self-discovery, is the central figure in the play. He is a middle-aged newspaperman "with a mysterious blank in his memory."[23] Long since separated from his parents and wife he is living in a bed-sitting room in Nottingham. Incapable of any deep felt human emotion, he is painfully aware of his inability to participate in the human situation. Like Querry, he also suffers from an absence of feeling. His wife is frightened by "his love of nothing": "You went looking for Nothing everywhere . . . I was jealous of Nothing as though it was a woman; and now you sleep with Nothing every night. . . .You're not alive. Sometimes I wanted to make you angry or sorry, to hurt you. But you never felt pain."[24] Greene presents the psychological emptiness of James very movingly. No longer in love with his wife, he bears a striking resemblance to Pyle of *The Quiet American* and Query of *A Burnt-out Case*, each with a difference. But most of all, he is like the little boy of "The Basement Room" who has now grown up. Deprived of the capability to love, James is a burnt-out case. He is keen to know the mystery of his being. His search begins after he is prevented from seeing his dying father. His mind is in torment when he is treated like a stranger in his parents' house. He is very anxious to know what's wrong with him, why do they keep him away. His search for the meaning of his lost blacked-out childhood becomes the primary concern of the writer.

As in *The Man Within*, James's feeling of non-existence is related to his childhood. His early upbringing in an austere gloomy ethos of rationalism has been stifling and uncongenial. His father, a staunch rationalist, earned his living by writing in support of his belief in the "empty universe", "uninhabited planets" and "coolings teller systems" and "the non-existence of Christian God". He discarded

God as a taboo. The child was attracted towards his uncle, a priest, who taught him to believe in the Crucifix. But his father forbade it. The priest says: "He was a very clever man . . . He took everything I told you and made fun of it. He made me a laughing stock before you. I had taught you about the virgin birth and he cured you with psychology . . . He was a bit too rough. A child can't stand confusion."[25] His mother too, modelled on Greene's mother, was a rationalist, cold and practical with a Fabian type of good sense. She was opposed to the supernatural and fairy stories which amuse children. She acted in "bad faith" and supported her husband knowing fully well that he was in the wrong. She did so against her intention: "He was someone I protected . . . It wasn't what I intended to be. But men either form us with their strength, or they form us with their weakness. They never let us be."[26] Mrs. Callifer preferred accommodating herself to the rationalist husband to caring for and loving her son. She says: "Henry was a fraud . . . One can love a fraud. Perhaps it's easier than loving rectitude."[27] Thus parents' strict discipline, their desire to bring up James along the modern lines and clash of loyalties led James to attempt suicide. Father Callifer remarks: "I was very angry with your father for the way he treated you. Of course he had reason, but it was a shocking thing for a boy to be brought to hang himself."[28]

The terrible event at the age of fourteen wiped out all memory. Now James does not remember anything beyond that illness. His miraculous recovery is a shock to the rationalists. It shakes his father's faith in the rational. Mrs. Callifer observes: "All his life he had written on the necessity of proof. Proof. And then a proof was pushed under his nose, at the bottom of his own garden, in the potting shed . . . I could hear him saying to himself, 'Must I recall all those books and start again'."[29]

Now he is caught up in a strange situation. He can't disbelieve the miracle and to admit a belief in it will spoil his public image. Moreover, it means to accept the pointlessness of his past life of a scientific rationalist. Throughout the remaining years of his life, he deliberately avoids meeting his son so as to combat what Colin Wilson calls "threshold consciousness" or "St Neot Margin" and in this he anticipates the Sculptor of *Carving a Statue*. The potter, who has seen the event, is pensioned off. James is kept aloof from him. His wife thinks it her duty to support him. Both of them, the husband and wife, together augment the anxiety of James instead of alleviating it. Mrs. Callifer herself admits: "Poor James had to suffer. We did him a great wrong. Henry and I. Why shouldn't he know—as much as we know?"[30]

They hide the mystery from James. When he insists on knowing his mother simply says: "We did not want you to remember how foolish you'd been. You were in a coma from shock. When the doctor came he revived you."[31]

In utter disappointment James voluntarily consults a psychoanalyst, Dr. Kreuzer, who fails to solve the mystery and who has no cure for the trouble of James. The doctor admits his failure: "I can only cure the irrational, the exaggerated, the abnormal. If a man is melancholy because he's lost his leg, I'm not called in. He has good reason."[32] Ann Callifer, a girl of thirteen, works like a detective and helps James to know the secret of his life. She reminds us of Coral Fellows of *The Power and the Glory*. Ann emphasizes the necessity of admitting the truth, of bringing to light the actions of the past so that they may lend meaning to the present and to the future. In this sense she is humanity, bright and alert. It is with her help that James comes in contact with Mrs. Potter and then his uncle Father William Callifer, who lays bare the facts of the past. James thus discovers himself and is reconciled to life and agrees to live with his wife. James's loss of memory and self-discovery insists on the illogicality of human life and the significance of self-knowledge and remind us of what Marlow says in *The Heart of Darkness*: "Droll thing life is—that mysterious arrangement of merciless logic for a futile purpose. The most you can hope from it is some knowledge of your self—that comes too late."[33]

The significance of self-knowledge which Greene has emphasized in the character of James reminds us of Dostoyevsky's statement in *The Brothers Karmazov*, I: "For the mystery of human life is not only in living, but in knowing why one lives. Without a clear idea of what to live for man will not consent to live and will rather destroy himself rather than remain on the earth, though he were surrounded by loaves of bread."[34]

The miracle that saves James has a very great effect on the various characters of the play. Father William Callifer's prayer, "Let him live, God. I love him. Let him live. . . take away what I love most. . . Take away my faith, but let him live,"[35] reminds us of Sarah's prayer to God in *The End of the Affair*. Sarah offers to believe in God if the lover were spared during the bombing raid. As Sarah leaps into faith, the priest leaps into unbelief. He spends many miserable and alcoholic years performing his duties without belief. He tries to find his faith again, but looks for it, as do the sisters in *The Living Room,* only in cheap religious pictures and conventional formulas. When he meets James, he is overwhelmed by the remembrance and truth of the miracle. He is never seen again, but one feels by the curtain of his scene that he gets his faith back. He says to James: "He answered my prayer. . . He took my offer. Look round you. Look at this room. It makes sense. . .I am tired and little drunk. I haven't thought about that day for thirty years."[36] In his meeting with his uncle, James acquires self-knowledge and is liberated from his late father's fearful and resentful attitude towards him. He admits, "The gap is filled. I know what happened."[37] In the last act he reawakens to the love, his wife still desires of him and agrees to live with her. He also confirms his faith in God. Faith is a paradox, which defeats logic and argument and defies human reason. There is no proof for the existence of God nor a proof that will satisfy a rationalist can be provided: "If I know I would not believe in Him. I couldn't believe in a God I could understand."[38] Uncle William's life without faith convinces James of the reality of God. He, like the little boy of the parable described in the story "The Hint of an Explanation", catches the hint of faith in his uncle's life without faith. Having seen his uncle, James does not "need any other proof of God than the lack of Him there".[39]

The miracle affects the rationalists too. James's father dares not stand face to face with the miracle. His mother frankly admits the truth, "You've spoilt our certainties."[40] Henry Callifer reminds us of Tolstoy's Karenin who is a thoroughly rationalist type, a dry and officious intellectual whose whole life has been constructed upon such rational precepts as to what one must be and do. But when he stands face to face with something illogical and irrational, he does not know what is to be done. Unwilling to accept the miracle, Dr. Batson, a true disciple of old Callifer, tries to manipulate it out of existence. He says, "I wouldn't accept a miracle. I would simply say we had to redefine our terms—the concepts life and death."[41]

The Potting Shed presents the age-old struggle between the rational and the vital. Greene who insists on the insufficiency of human reason to grasp the mysterious elements of man's existence seems to be on the side of the vital. He attempts to see the whole integral man in place of the rational fragment of him. If reason succumbs to its own hubris and denies that the supernatural exists, it only contrives to flee from the self. Reason may veil the truth of life. Greene stresses the need of accepting both, the rational and the vital. The "Potting Shed" is a place of hope to be acknowledged and accepted and not to be feared and shunned.

As *The Living Room* criticizes superstition and blind adherence to the conventional piety, *The Potting Shed* denounces the modern tendency to over-emphasize the rationalist standpoint. It insists on man's freedom of faith and the irrelevance of scientific proof for the existence of God.

The Complaisant Lover is a comedy whereas the previous plays were serious. Greene writes in the Preface to the collected edition of his works for the stage, "The strain of writing a novel, which keeps the author confined for a period of years with his depressive self, is extreme, and I have always sought relief in "entertainments"—for melodrama as much as farce is an expression of a manic mood. So with my third play I sought my usual escape."[42] Though this play stays within the narrow range of urban domesticity, it is concerned with the same values which are found in the earlier plays and has something just as important to say about them.

The play offers Greene's critical and scornful outlook on the modern tendency to have a specialized profession. The elaborate sub-divisions of human functions which is characteristic of the present century requires expert knowledge and know-how. The price people pay for having a profession is a *d'formation professionale*, as the French put it—a professional deformation. Professional people tend to see things from the viewpoint of their own speciality and usually show a very marked blind spot to whatever falls outside this particular province.

Victor Rhodes, the main figure in the play, is a dentist having professional narrowness. A dentist in Greene is a symbol of pain, emptiness and indifference. Victor reminds us of Tench, the dentist in *The Power and the Glory*. Victor, a man with a sense of humour and too many anecdotes, is a bore to his attractive wife as well as to his friends. His preoccupation with his work estranges him from his wife and children. When he talks to his wife, he talks about household affairs—the repair or repainting of rooms, health and education of children—and most often bed-time is the only chance when the husband and wife talk because "Dentists are very busy men."[43] Sick of daily routine life, his wife starts an affair with Clive Root, the owner of an antiquarian bookshop, to tide over the feeling of her boredom. During his trip to Amsterdam, Victor is busy "looking particularly for some new instruments for gingivectomy"[44] and finds no time to take his wife for sight-seeing. He is so possessed by his work that he is not able to guess any evil about his wife even after seeing Clive walking into her bed-room before she is dressed: "Victor's a damned wise monkey. He sees no evil, thinks no evil."[45] For him, it is not a holiday. It's work. "There's always work."[46] He never feels free. He looks at things from the viewpoint of his profession and "brings dentistry into everything",[47] even in ordinary conversation he draws comparison from the vocabulary commonly used in his job. He compares early friends to milk teeth, for they "drop out like milk teeth".[48] His talk about his job at home disgusts his wife who out of annoyance asks him to leave dentistry in surgery. But he can't help, it's his life, even his "letters are dental".[49] He feels lost when out of his surgery and, like Tench of *The Power and the Glory*, he takes great pride in his professional skill. He knows all that is required for a dentist—surgery, radiology and prosthesis: "I have attained certain position in my life. There are not many men in my profession I would acknowledge as my masters."[50] But he has a feeling that his profession is not a glamorous one and people look at it with contempt: ". . . .My patients don't ask us to dinner. Yet they ask their doctor. Though he deals in more ignoble parts of the body than I do."[51]

The play offers Greene's concept of Christian marriage. Marriage is a permanent union of man and woman. It is a bond that is more complex than just sex and it grows with the years with children, with the kind of understanding that has to develop between people who go through that round together. Victor and Mary have lived together in perfect understanding between them since their marriage sixteen years ago. Boredom has set in. The husband is now sexually impotent. Age has killed his desire for sex. Mary says: ". . . we have not slept together for five years. . . When that dies out, Clive, it doesn't come back. And sooner or later it always dies. Even for us it would die in time. It dies quicker in a marriage, that's all. It's killed by the children, by the chars who give notice, by the price of meat."[52] The boredom of domestic life leads to a tension between the husband and the wife. Mary finds herself in a strange situation, like the lovers in *The Living Room*. She is torn by a conflict between her desire for happiness and duty. She desires to live happily in years to come with her lover; on the other hand she feels responsibility for her husband and children. She says to Victor: "I don't want to choose. I don't want to leave you and the children. I don't want to leave him. Victor, dear Victor, why can't we sometimes, just once, have our cake and eat it."[53] This is the nature of life. It is illogical. There is discrepancy between desire and its fulfilment. The play makes no specific reference to religion. The husband-wife relationship proves vital and the family is preserved. Victor and Mary are free individuals. The thought of sexual violation or any consideration for traditional morality does not affect their choice. They are merely concerned with the need of their existence. Their existential freedom entails a sense of responsibility for the children. Victor urges Mary to stay with him because he needs her. He at the same time understands the problem of his wife. He realizes: "She has no work except the family round. Children, servants, meals—it's not a real vocation. And so to make up she has to have —well, I'd call them illusions."[54]

Hence he agrees to be a complaisant husband and asks Clive to remain a complaisant lover. He throws out a suggestion to the satisfaction of all the three to carry on their affairs at a distance. Thus the play points out that love is not just sex. When sex is asleep or gone, love can go on growing. Marriage is "living in the same house with someone you love".[55] Boredom is a part of it. One has to put up with it. Life itself is boring: "The trouble about marriage is, it's a damned boring condition even with a lover. Boredom is not a good reason for changing a profession or a marriage."[56] Marriage is a condition that preserves values that matter and endure and keeps them alive so that they can survive the physical changes brought about by advancing years.

The concept of marriage presented here reminds one of Kierkegaard who in *Either/Or* explores the nature of decision with special reference to three cases—marriage, friendship and vocation. Marriage, Kierkegaard thinks, is a life-long union of two persons who commit themselves to each other for better or for worse, a relationship that utterly transcends any temporary mood or infatuation: "Husband and wife promise to love one another for eternity. . . If marriage has reality, then he is sufficiently punished by forfeiting this happiness; if it has no reality, it is absurd to abuse him because he is wiser than the rest."[57] In this play Greene comes very close to Kierkegaard in insisting on the spirit of marriage and not on its form. Both husband and wife freely decide to stay together as they need each other, the form of the marriage does not affect their choice. They are governed by self-law and hence Greene's emphasis on the worth and dignity of the individual.

Thus Greene's theme in *The Complaisant Lover* is man's feeling of alienation and boredom arising from the divisions of human functions requiring expert knowledge and technical skill. The play records Greene's protest against the conventional standards of morality and emphasizes man's existential freedom that involves his responsibility for others.

Carving a Statue, Greene's last attempt for the theatre, is a far more serious play than *The Complaisant Lover*. It raises issues similar to those raised in the previous plays. Greene's main theme in *Carving a Statue* is the feeling of despair and a lack of human relationship between a sculptor and his son. The sculptor, like Victor of *The Complaisant Lover*, is obsessed—to the sacrifice of any personal life—by the desire to erect a statue of God the Father and is "too busy to care"[58] for his fifteen-year-old son who is anxious to learn how to lead his own life. He reminds us of James of *The Potting Shed.*

The sculptor truly represents the twentieth-century man. He is seized with the painful feeling of anxiety which lies in his inability to deal with the threat of a special situation, that is his wife's death. Unable to bear the sight of his wife's death, as he informs his son, he "ran out of the room before the breathing stopped".[59] In his anxiety about the special situation is also implied the anxiety about human situation. Since his wife's death he has been running away from life as he is not able to encounter its reality. He "cannot take life except at second-hand"[60] and so he is anxious to be another self. His dedication to recreating God is a means to escape life and its suffering—"The statue is a cave"[61] where he hides and the image of God he builds mirrors "his retreat from life into egoism".[62] As long as he works, he holds "the pain of the world away"[63] from himself. His son, on the other hand, potters solitarily in the workshop, fetching him tea, spam and guinness and feels alienated from his father. He is anxious to see his father as "an ordinary man",[64] who could explain things to him at home. Unfortunately, he is left to work out everything from the beginning for himself and suffers from a feeling of boredom and loneliness and seeks riddance through sex and love and is robbed of both. The child reminds us of Greene's own boyhood when he experienced a deep sense of abandonment in his parent's home—father shut in his study working on the time-table of the school and mother detached from children by the presence of a host of servants.

The sculptor's obsession has dehumanized him. The sap of life is dried up and he is incapable of natural love and affection. Like his friend, Dr. Parker, who after telling reassuring stories to his frightened patients becomes "a block of stone indifferent to human suffering",[65] the sculptor "knows all about indifference . . . and nothing about love".[66] Greene shows through the figures of the sculptor and his son that anxiety is existential and it cannot be removed. The sculptor is terribly struck with the anxiety of feeling guilty and the horror of feeling condemned when his son, with the dead body of the deaf, dumb and blind girl in his arms, helplessly implores: "Father! She's dead. Come out of there and speak to me, father. I'm alone, I need you. Help me. I'm your son."[67] Shaken and horrified by the pitiable sight, the sculptor has a moment of insight into himself: "Pain teaches quickly. I'm frightened of pain."[68] But his desire to escape pain and suffering is not shattered permanently. The experience is just a shocking inconvenience and not suffering felt from the whole being. The awareness of real guilt and the horror of self-condemnation, which is identical with man's existential self-estrangement, are repressed because the courage which would take them into itself is lacking. His work proves to be an effective means of combating what Colin Wilson calls threshold consciousness or "St. Neot Margin". His obsession returns: "All I've done is not wasted. I can start again."[69]

Greene emphasizes the necessity of fulfilling the need of children which is most often neglected in our time. The sculptor belongs to the class of villains in Greene, who deprive children and do not care for their needs. They include James's parents in *The Potting Shed*, Philip's parents in the story "The Basement Room", Andrews's in *The Man Within* and Anthony's father in *England Made Me*. Greene points out that a man neglected in childhood feels lost in later life. Thus the theme of the play is despair. The sculptor despairs of willing to be another self whereas his son despairs of willing his own self. They suffer from a deep sense of alienation from which man suffers in modern busy life.

This brief survey of the plays leads us to conclude that Greene's main concern here, as elsewhere, is the existential freedom of the individual. Greene is totally opposed to the systems that restrict man's freedom. In *The Living Room*, he denounces the formalities of the church which impair the vision of the elderly women and cripple the priest's response to his conscienee. *The Potting Shed* condemns the rational outlook of the Callifers, which has alienated them from their son and lays stress on faith which is irrational. In *The Complaisant Lover*, Greene insists on the alienating effect of a specialized profession and underlines the significance of the individual's free and untrammelled decision with regard to marriage. *Carving a Statue* develops the themes of *The Potting Shed* and *The Complaisant Lover*. It examines how the preoccupation of a man destroys his existence, devalues his worth and dignity as an individual and erodes the natural relationship between a father and a son. Thus the plays emphasize Greene's love for the individual and hatred for anything that corrupts and destroys his individuality.

Notes and References

1. Graham Greene, *Three Plays* (London: Mercury Books, 1961), p. X.
2. "Then I attempted the theatre: first modestly enough with one act plays, very tragic and very brutal set in the Middle Ages. . .", *A Sort of Life*, p. 80.
3. *Three Plays*, p. XIII.
4. Graham Greene, *The Living Room* (London: William Heinemann, 1953), Penguin Books, 1970, pp. 30-1.
5. *Ibid.*, p. 61.
6. *Ibid.*, p. 54.
7. *Ibid.*
8. *Ibid.*, p. 74.
9. *Ibid.*
10. *Ibid.*, p. 42.
11. *Ibid.*, pp. 45-6.
12. *Ibid.*, p. 46.
13. *Ibid.*, p. 60.
14. *Ibid.*, p. 63.
15. *Ibid.*, p. 73.
16. *Ibid.*, pp. 74-5.
17. *The End of the Affair*, p. 191.
18. *The Living Room*, p. 82.
19. Gabriel Marcel, *The Philosophy of Existence*, p. 15.
20. Greene's personal letter, March 6, 1978.
21. James Joxon, "Kierkegaard's Stages and *A Burnt-out Case*", *Review of English Literature*, 3 (1962), 92.
22. *A Sort of Life*, pp. 137-38.
23. Martin Browne, "Graham Greene: Theatre's Gain", *Theatre Arts*, 45, November 1961, p. 21.
24. Graham Greene, *The Potting Shed* (London: William Heinemann Ltd., 1957), Penguin Books, 1971, p. 26.
25. *Ibid.*, p. 72.
26. *Ibid.*, pp. 35-6.
27. *Ibid.*, p. 79.
28. *Ibid.*, p. 73.
29. *Ibid.*, p. 80.
30. *Ibid.*, p. 28.
31. *Ibid.*, p. 63.
32. *Ibid.*, p. 52.
33. *The Heart of Darkness*, p. 100.
34. *The Brothers Karmazov*, I, p. 298.
35. *The Potting Shed*, p. 75.
36. *Ibid.*
37. *Ibid.*, p. 83.
38. *Ibid.*, p. 84.
39. *Ibid.*, p. 88.
40. *Ibid.*, p. 89.
41. *Ibid.*, p. 81.
42. Graham Greene, *Three Plays*, p. XIII.
43. Graham Greene, *The Complaisant Lover* (London: William Heinemann Ltd., 1959), Penguin Books, 1971, p. 28.

44. *Ibid.*, p. 50.
45. *Ibid.*, p. 54.
46. *Ibid.*, p. 73.
47. *Ibid.*, p. 39.
48. *Ibid.*
49. *Ibid.*, p. 67.
50. *Ibid.*, p. 12.
51. *Ibid.*, p. 36.
52. *Ibid.*, pp. 27-8.
53. *Ibid.*, p. 85.
54. *Ibid.*, p. 88.
55. *Ibid.*, p. 71.
56. *Ibid.*
57. S. Kierkegaard, *Either/Or: A Fragment of Life*, trans. W. Lowrie (Princeton: Princeton University Press, 1944), pp. 243-44.
58. Graham Greene, *Carving a Statue* (London: Bodley Head, 1964), Penguin Books, 1972, p. 41.
59. *Ibid.*, p. 79.
60. *Ibid.*
61. *Ibid.*, p. 78.
62. Ronald Bryden, "Some bodaddy", *New Statesman*, September 25, 1964, p. 462.
63. *Carving a Statue*, p. 79.
64. *Ibid.*, p. 20.
65. *Ibid.*, p. 61.
66. *Ibid.*, p. 79.
67. *Ibid.*, p. 78.
68. *Ibid.*, p. 79.
69. *Ibid.*, p. 80.

Conclusion

IN his novels, stories and plays discussed in the preceding chapters, Graham Greene faithfully renders the modern mood of anxiety and boredom and man's isolation in an alien universe. Like the existentialists, he protests against the moral and spiritual degradation of man in our age. He is full of indignation with the "advanced" societies in which man suffers from a feeling of estrangement and "lostness", of "sickness unto death" caused by the complexities of modern life—mechanization, urbanization, State administration and propaganda—which he can neither avoid nor control. Scientific experiments and new discoveries made in the various walks of life have, without doubt, multiplied the sources of man's pleasure and comfort, but they have also reduced the significance of man as a spiritual being. Man today seems to have lost his way in the dark, because neither within him nor without does he find anything to cling to. Greene himself suffered from total and perpetual boredom and came to terms with his life by his own efforts. His characters, too, are angst-ridden because they are incapable of being at one with their deeper selves. Like Greene himself, his protagonists, like Scobie, Querry and Castle, seem to be sick with the disease of modern civilization and have to search for the meaning of life in the dark and distant solitudes of Africa. Disillusioned with the technological culture of our times, Greene sadly feels that man has suffered a loss in terms of "the finer taste, the finer pleasure and the finer terror"[1] that the African natives have at their command. He writes in his *In Search of a Character*: "How strange it is that for more than a hundred years Africa has been recommended as a cure for the sick heart."[2] Though Greene has no desire to stay in Africa nor he yearns for a mindless sensuality which may be found there, Greene feels that "when one has appreicated such a beginning, its terror as well as placidity, the power as well as the gentleness, the pity for what we have done with ourselves is driven more forcibly home".[3]

Greene is very well aware of the liberal progressive outlook prevailing in our age that believes in the improvement of life through various welfare provisions. But they fall short of the need of man who is a citizen of two worlds, spiritual as well as material. Greene, naturally, minimizes the importance of systems established by the lovers of humanity for the happiness of mankind and deprecates the modern habit of reducing the whole range of human satisfactions to averages of statistical figures and scientifico-economic formulas. He is inclined to believe that prosperity is not the only thing that pleases and satisfies mankind. Sometimes a man like the Priest, Scobie or Querry is intensely, even passionately, attached to suffering. In spite of all earthly blessings, comforts and economic prosperity, man sometimes deliberately longs for the most uneconomic nonsense. Perhaps suffering is just as good for man as comfort and prosperity. Greene appears to be of the view that man will be "happier with the enormous supernatural promise than with the petty social fulfilment, the tiny pension and the machine-made furniture".[4] Like his protagonists, the Priest, Scobie and Querry, Greene believes in the ubiquity of pain and suffering in human life and insists on the significance of man's spiritual satisfaction. Scobie appears to be voicing Greene's own view when he says that to be a human being one must "drink the cup".[5]

Greene repudiates the modern emphasis on unalloyed rationalism. His works show that reason alone cannot solve life's most central problems. Contemporary disorder has grown in spite of all beautiful systems and theories explaining man's best interests. The extension of rationality or the heightening of the intellectuality of man's perception, which is counted as human progress today, is little short of sophistry. Greene thinks that the advance of man's intellectuality at the expense of his spontaneous life may generate a dangerous and explosive recoil in man and society. Man has an inner being which is beyond the reach of human intellect. Greene believes in the force of the irrational which is impenetrable through man's intelligence. Life is a mystery which is neither intelligible nor manageable. The part of life which is predictable is just a fragment of an inaccesssible whole. The key to a full understanding of the part of the world accessible to man through his senses (including introspection) and through scientific thought working on sense-data, lies in the other part not accessible in this way. Greene writes in an essay entitled "The Explorers: "Men have always tried to rationalize their irrational acts, but the explanations given in prospectuses like those of the South Sea Bubble and the African Association are as unconvincing as last night's supper as the cause of our fantastic dreams."[6]

In *The Honorary Consul* Dr. Plarr gives a positive reason for rejecting the optimistic view of Dr. Saavedra: "Life isn't like that. Life is not noble or dignified. . . Nothing is ineluctable. Life has surprises. Life is absurd."[7] Further implication of such an attitude becomes explicit in Greene's statement, "In a commercial world of profit and loss man is often hungry for the irrational."[8] In one of his essays, Greene bewails the sudden and inexplicable shattering of the old world with all its faiths and values and the creation of a moral vacuum which is filled by violence. This is something which he cannot understand: "There are things one never gets used to because they don't connect: sanctity and fidelity and the courage of human beings abandoned to free will: virtues like these belong with old college buildings and cathedrals, relics of a world with faith. Violence comes to us more easily because it was so long expected—not only by the political sense but by the moral sense."[9] His stories in *A Sense of Reality* and his novels *Brighton Rock*, *The Power and the Glory* *The Heart of the Matter*, *The End of the Affair* and the play *The Potting Shed*, offer Greene's criticism of the modern tendency to fit every aspect of life which might be confusing into some intellectual scheme and reveal his attraction towards the irrational in life.

Greene's religious novels, *Brighton Rock*, *The Power and the Glory*, *The Heart of the Matter* and *The End of the Affair*, and his plays, *The Living Room* and *The Potting Shed*, are mainly concerned with the paradoxical nature of faith. To Greene, faith is the recoil from the uttér despair of unbelief. James, the crippled priest of *The Living Room*, appears to be speaking for Greene himself when he says that "The more our senses are revolted, uncertain and in despair, the more surely Faith says: 'This is God: all goes well'."[10] Faith has to do with just this—with the hardness, the impossibility, even absurdity of belief in the absence of objective evidence. It is a sudden leap into the unknown. To make movements of faith one must shut one's eyes and plunge confidently into the absurd and take the risk of jumping into the abyss. Self-knowledge is more relevant to faith than reason. If one has established proof then there is no longer anything to believe in, no longer any occasion for faith. Faith is an act of will and of choice. Knowledge of God is an inward experience. If the approach has not been made, proofs are irrelevant. Proofs will not produce or conjure up God. Greene has a suspicion of organized religion. Prayer, baptism and confession are no aid to faith. Greene is always impatient with the church as an organization insisting upon the unquestioning faith in its dogmas. Like Kierkegaard's Abraham and Mary whose faith did not free them from hardship, Greene's characters share his own persistent agony of mind, which must be endured by all who feel torn between a natural need for a minimum of human happiness and the exacting demands of faith. Greene insists on man's freedom of faith. He writes in *The Lawless Roads*: "And so faith came to one—shapelessly, without dogma, a presence above a croquet lawn, something associated with violence, cruelty, evil across the way. One began to believe in heaven because one believed in hell, but for a long while it was only hell one could picture with a certain intimacy."[11] This view places Greene in the company of Christian existentialists like Kierkegaard, Marcel, Buber and Paul Tillich. To Paul Tillich, "Faith includes both an immediate awareness of something unconditional and the courage to take the risk of uncertainty upon itself. Faith says, 'Yes' in spite of the anxiety of 'No'. It does not remove the 'no' of doubt and the anxiety of doubt".[12] Similarly, faith, according to Marcel, must triumph over "the state of self-division"[13] which constitutes the existence of a finite being. Though faith spontaneously springs from man's internal resources, it is not arbitrary. Greene, like the Christian existentialists, believes in the interdependence of human and divine love. His works reveal that human love is a prerequisite to divine love. Before realizing divine love, *agape*, a man must suffer human love, as Greene's protagonists do.

In his secular novels, Greene seeks to arrive at a positive meaning of life through the realization of the absurd. He denies absolute morality and tries to establish instead that man creates his own meaning. He shows that man is responsible for what he is and what he does. At the same time, he is responsible for the entire mankind. Greene's preoccupation with the search for ethics in the absence of God brings him close to Sartre. Like Sartre, Greene graphically presents the two modes of action—action rising from man's direct personal experience and action inspired by an abstract ideal. He points out that commitment to a course of action without personal or emotional involvement is absurd and outmoded. Communism or any other ideology is unlikely to bring about any appreciable improvement in the situation because plans and projects, however good those may bə, prove disastrous on account of their utopian elements and frequent changes in the social and political systems. Greene insists on man's existential freedom that burdens him with responsibilities for others.

In his search for a way of life which will preserve the worth and dignity of the individual in a materialistic society, Greene travels from the commercial and Godless world of his earlier novels where the individual, a sad, solitary figure, is groping in the dark, to the world of the religious novels where the individual is torn by the inner struggle ensuing from his spiritual hunger and an agonized sense of life, and thence to the world of the secular novels where the individual, like Maurice Castle of *The Human Factor*, is anxious to "find a permanent home, in a city where he could be accepted as a citizen, as a citizen without any pledge of faith, not the city of God or Marx, but the city called Peace of Mind".[14] Though like Sarah of *The End af the Affair*, Greene has "caught belief, like a disease",[15] its best expression lies in a concern for man. His themes turn on the fate of individuals caught in a system and underline the horror of violence in a landscape of war, hot and cold, economic depression, revolution, espionage and counter-espionage, racial prejudices and apartheid. His protagonists are isolated, disillusioned, defeated and destroyed, and Greene appears to be averse to offering facile solutions to the plight of the contemporary man. However, Greene has successfully understood the predicament in which man finds himself today and his heroes, who are trapped in an existential web and who create their own beings, are shown to have discovered, even in their isolation, disillusionment, defeat or death, some positive values of life like love, nobility, dignity and authenticity. While voicing his protest against some of the traditional faiths and ideals, Greene seeks to salvage the others giving them additional humanistic or even existential dimensions.

Notes and References

1. Graham Greene, *Journey Without Maps*, p. 226.
2. Graham Greene, *In Search of a Character*: *Two African Journals* (London: Bodley Head, 1961), Penguin Books, 1968, p. 27.
3. *Journey Without Maps*, p. 249.
4. *The Lawless Roads*, p. 49.
5. *The Heart of the Matter*, p. 118.
6. Graham Greene, *Collected Essays* (London: Bodley Head, 1969), Penguin Books, 1977, p. 237.
7. *The Honorary Consul*, p. 16.
8. Graham Greene, "A Letter to a German Friend", *New Statesman*, May 31, 1963, p. 824.
9. Graham Greene, *Collected Essays*, p. 334.
10. *The Living Room*, p. 80.
11. *The Lawless Roads*, p. 16.
12. Paul Tillich, *Biblical Religion and the Search for Reality* (Chicago: The University of Chicago Press, 1955), p. 61.
13. *Metaphysical Journal*, p. 225.
14. *The Human Factor*, p. 107.
15. *The End of the Affair*, p. 147.

Select Bibliography

Primary Sources

Greene, Graham, *Babbling April*, Oxford, 1925.

—, *The Man Within*, London: Heinemann, 1929, Penguin Books, 1971.

—, *The Name of Action*, London: Heinemann, 1930 (withdrawn).

—, *Rumour at Nightfall*, London: Heinemann, 1931 (withdrawn).

—, *Stamboul Train*, London: Heinemann, 1932, Penguin Books, 1963.

—, *It's a Battlefield*, London: Heinemann, 1934, Penguin Books, 1971.

—, *England Made Me*, London: Heinemann, 1935, Penguin Books, 1970.

—, *A Gun For Sale*, London: Heinemann, 1936, Penguin Books, 1977.

—, *Journey Without Maps*, London: Heinemann, 1936, Penguin Books, 1971.

—, *Brighton Rock*, London: Heinemann, 1938, Penguin Books, 1974.

—, *The Confidential Agent*, London: Heinemann, 1939, Penguin Books, 1963.

—, *The Lawless Roads*, London: Heinemann, 1939, Penguin Books, 1976.

—, *The Power and the Glory*, London: Heinemann, 1940, Penguin Books, 1974.

—, *The Minisry of Fear*, London: Heinemann, 1943, Penguin Books, 1976.

—, *The Heart of the Matter*, London: Heinemann, 1948, Penguin Books, 1970.

—, *Why Do I Write?* An Exchange of Views Between Elizabeth Bowen, Greene and V.S. Prichett, New York, 1948.

—, *The Third Man*, London: Heinemann, 1950, Penguin Books, 1977.

—, *The End of the Affair*, London: Heinemann, 1951, Penguin Books, 1975.

—, *The Living Room*, London: Heinemann, 1953, Penguin Books, 1970.

—, *Twenty-one Short Stories*, London: Heinemann, 1954, Penguin Books, 1970.

—, *The Quiet American*, London: Heinemann, 1955, Penguin Books, 1973.

—, *Loser Takes All*, London: Heinemann, 1955, Penguin Books, 1971.

—, *The Potting Shed*, London: Heinemann, 1958, Penguin Books, 1971.

—, *Our Man in Havana*, London: Heinemann, 1958.

—, *The Complaisant Lover*, London: Heinemann, 1959, Penguin Books, 1971.

—, *In Search of a Character: Two African Journals*, London: Bodley Head, 1961, Penguin Books, 1968.

—, *A Sense of Reality*, London: Heinemann, 1963, Penguin Books, 1968.

—, *Carving a Statue*, London: Heinemann, 1964, Penguin Books, 1973.

—, *The Comedians*, London: Bodley Head, 1966, Penguin Books, 1975.

—, *May We Borrow Your Husband and Other Comedies Sexual of Life*, London: Heinemann, 1967.

—, *Travels With My Aunt*, London: Bodley Head, 1969, Penguin Books, 1971.

—, *Collected Essays*, London: Bodley Head, 1969, Penguin Books, 1970.

—, *A Sort of Life*, London: Bodley Head, 1971, Penguin Books, 1972.

—, *The Honorary Consul*, London: Bodley Head, 1973, Penguin Books, 1974.

—, *The Human Factor*, London: Bodley Head, 1978, Penguin Books, 1978.

Secondary Sources

(A) Books

Allen, Edgar L., *Existentialism From Within*, London: Routledge and Kegan Paul, 1953.

Allen, Walter, "Graham Greene", *Writers of Today*, ed., Denysval Baker, London: Sidgwick and Jackson, 1965.
—, *Tradition and Dream*, Penguin Books, 1965.
—, *The English Novel*, Penguin Books, 1954.
Allott, Kenneth and Miriam Farris, *The Art of Graham Greene*, London: Hamish Hamilton, 1951.
Allott, Miriam, *Novelists on the Novel*, London: Routledge and Kegan Paul, 1962.
Atkins, John, *Graham Greene*, London: John Calder, 1957.
Augustine, St., *The Confessions of St. Augustine*, trans. Sir Tobie Matthew Collins, London: Fontana Books, 1963.
Barnes, Hazel E., *The Literature of Possibility: A Study in Humanistic Existentialism*, Lincoln: University of Nebraska Press, 1959.
Barret, William, *Irrational Man: A Study in Existential Philosophy*, London: Mercury Books, 1960.
Beach, J.W., *The Twentieth Century Novel*, Lyall Book Depot, 1965.
Beckett, S., *Malone Dies*, London: Calder and Byrons, 1958, Penguin Books, 1977.
—, *Murphy*, London: Calder and Byrons, 1969.
—, *Waiting For Godot*, London: Faber and Faber Limited, 1956.
Bergonzi, B., *The Situation of the Novel*, Pennsylvania: University of Pittsburgh, 1971.
—, *The Holy Bible*, London: British and Foreign Bible Society.
Blackham, H.J., *Six Existentialist Thinkers*, New York: Harper and Row, 1959.
Boardman, G.R., *Graham Greene: The Aesthetic Exploration*, University of Florida Press, 1971.
Bobbio, N., *The Philosophy of Decadentism: A Study in Existentialism*, trans. David Moore, Oxford: Basil Blackwell, 1948.
Booth, Wayne, C., *The Rhetoric of Fiction*, Chicago: University of Chicago Press, 1961.
Bretall, Robert, *Kierkegaard Anthology*, ed., London: N.U.P., 1947.
Browne, E.M., "Contemporary Drama in the Catholic Tradition", *Christian Faith and the Contemporary Arts*, ed. F. Eversole, Nashville, 1962.
Buber, Martin, *I and Thou*, trans. R.G. Smith, 2nd Ed., New York: Charles Scribner's Sons, 1958.
Bultman, R., *Jesus Christ and Mythology*, trans. R.H. Fuller, New York: Charles Scribner's Sons, 1958.
Burgess, A., *The Novel Now*, London: Faber and Faber Ltd., 1967.

—, *Devil of a State*, London: Heinemann, 1961.

Calderwood, J.L., and Harold, E.T., *Perspectives of Fiction*, ed., New York: O.U.P., 1968.

Camus, A., *The Plague*, trans. Stuart Gilbert, Hamish Hamilton, 1948, Penguin Books, 1976.

—, *The Fall*, trans. Justin O'Brien, London: Hamish Hamilton, 1957, Penguin Books, 1976.

—, *A Happy Death*, trans. Richard Howard, London: Hamish Hamilton, 1972, Penguin Books, 1976.

—, *Exile and Kingdom*, trans. Justin O'Brien, London: Hamish Hamilton, 1958, Penguin Books, 1975.

—, *The Myth of Sisyphus*, trans. Justin O'Brien, London: Hamish Hamilton, 1955, Penguin Books, 1977.

—, *The Rebel: An Essay on Man in Revolt*, trans. A. Bower, London: Hamish Hamilton, 1956, Penguin Books, 1973.

—, *Caligula and Cross Purposes*, Penguin Books, 1965.

Cargas, H.J., *Graham Greene*, ed. Christian Critic Series, St. Louis, 1969.

Chapman, R., "The Vision of Greene", *Forms of Extremity in the Modern Novel*, ed., N.A. Scott, Richmondva, 1965.

Chiari, Joseph, *Realism and Imagination*, London: Barrie and Rockliff, 1960.

Church, R., *British Authors*, London: Longmans, 1943.

Collins, A.S., *English Literature of the Twentieth Century*, London: University Tutorial Press, 1956.

Comer Chero, V., *Values in Conflict: Christianity Marxism, Psychoanalysis, Existentialism*, New York: Appleton-Century Crofts, 1970.

Quickshank, John, *Albert Camus and the Literature of Revolt*, New York: O.U.P., 1966.

Conrad, J., *The Heart of Darkness*, J.M. Dent and Sons, 1902, Penguin Books, 1975.

—, *Lord Jim*, J.M. Dent and Sons, 1900, Penguin Books, 1976.

—, *The Secret Agent*, J.M. Dent and Sons, 1907, Penguin Books, 1974.

—, *Under Western Eyes*, J.M. Dent and Sons, 1911, Penguin Books, 1957.

—, *Victory*, J.M. Dent and Sons, 1915, Penguin Books, 1974.

D'Arcy, Martin, *The Mind and Heart of Love*, New York: Meridian Books, 1956.

Daiches, David, *The Novel and the Modern World*, Chicago: University of Chicago Press, 1964.

Davis, R. Graham, *Highlights of Modern Literature*, ed. Francis Brown, New York: Mentor Books, 1954.

DeVitis, A.A., *Graham Greene*, New York: Twayne Publishers, 1964.

Dostoyevsky, F., *The Brothers Karamazov*, trans. Magarshack, Hazell Watson and Viney Limited, 1958, Penguin Books, 1976.

—, *Notes From Underground*, trans. Jessie Coulson, Cox and Wyman Ltd., 1972, Penguin Books, 1977.

Eastman, R.M., *A Guide to the Novel*, Pennsylvania: Candlu Publishing Company, 1965.

Esslin, Martin, *The Theatre of the Absurd*, Penguin Books, 1977.

Evans, R.O., *Graham Greene: Some Critical Considerations*, ed. Lexington: University of Kentucky Press, 1967.

Fraser, G.S., *The Modern Writer and His World*, London: Penguin Books, 1964.

Follico, A.B., *Art and Existentialism*, New York: Prentice Hall, 1962.

Forster, E.M., *Aspects of the Novel*, London: Edward Arnold, 1953.

Friedman, Alan, *The Twentieth Century Mind*, ed. C.B. Cox and A.E., Dyson, London: O.U.P., 1972.

Gassner, J., "Points of Return: Religion and Greene's *The Potting Shed*", *Theatre at the Crossroads*, New York, 1960.

Ghent, Dorothy Van, *The English Novel: Form and Function*, New York: Holt Rinehart and Winston, 1953.

Golding. William, *Free Fall*, London: Faber and Faber, 1968.

—, *Lord of the Flies*, London: Faber and Faber, 1954.

Hall, J., "Efficient Saints and Civilians: Greene", *Lunatic Giant in the Drawing Room*, Bloomington, 1968.

Hartley, L.P., *The Novelist's Responsibility*, London: Hamish Hamilton, 1967.

Harvey, A.J., *Character and the Novel*, London: Chatto and Windus, 1966.

Heidegger, M., *Being and Time*, trans. J. Macquarrie and E.S. Robinson, New York: Harper and Row, 1962.

Heinemann, M.W., *Existentialism and the Modern Predicament*, New York: Harper and Brothers, 1958.

Hoggart, Richard., *The Uses of Literacy*, London: Chatto and Windus, 1959.

Hynes, Samuel, *Graham Greene: A Collection of Critical Essays*, New York: Prentice Hall, 1973.

James, W., *The Varieties of Religious Experience*, New York: Mentor Books, 1958.

Jaspers, K., *Man in the Modern Age*, trans. Eden and Cedar Paul, New York: Doubleday, 1956.

Joselyn, M., "Greene's Novels: the Conscience in the World", *Literature and Society*, ed. B. Slote, Lincoln Nebr, 1964.

John of the Cross, St., *The Complete Works of St. John of the Cross*, London: Burns and Oates, 1967.

—, *The Dark Night of the Soul*, London: Thomas Baker, 1916.

Kafka, F., *The Great Wall of China*, trans. Willa and Edwin Muir, London: Martin Secker and Warburg, 1946.

—, *The Castle*, trans, Willa Edwin Muir, Penguin Books, 1976.

—, *The Trial*, trans. Willa and Edwin Muir, Penguin Books, 1976.

—, *Metamorphosis and Other Stories*, trans. Willa and Edwin Muir, Penguin Books, 1976.

Karl, F.R., *A Reader's Guide to Contemporary English Novel*, London: Thames and Hudson, 1964.

Kaufmann, Walter, *Existentialism from Dostoyevsky to Sartre*, Cleveland and New York: Meridian Books, The World Publishing Company, 1968.

Kazin, A., *Contemporaries*. Boston: Little Brown and Co., 1962.

Kermode, Frank, *Puzzles and Epiphanies*, London: Routledge and Kegan Paul, 1962.

Kettle, Arnold, *An Introduction to the English Novel*, II, London: Arrow Books, 1962.

Kierkegaard, S., *The Concept of Dread*, trans. Walter Lowrie, Princeton: Princeton University Press, 1944.

—, *Concluding Unscientific Postscript*, trans. D.F. Swenson, Princeton: Princeton University Press, 1941.

—, *Fear and Trembling and The Sickness Unto Death*, trans. Walter Lowrie, New York; Doubleday, 1954.

—, *Either/Or: A Fragment of Life*, trans. W. Lowrie, Princeton: Princeton University Press, 1944.

Kohn, L., *Greene: The Major Novels*, Stanford, 1961.

Kunkel, F.L., *The Labyrinthine Ways of Greene*, New York, 1960.

Kulshrestha, J.P., *Graham Greene the Novelist*, Madras: The Macmillan Company of India Ltd., 1977.

Lebowitz, N., *Humanism and the Absurd in the Modern Novel*, Illinois: North Western University Press, 1971.

Lewis, R.W.B., *The Picaresque Saint*, London: Victor Collanez, 1960.

Lehn, R., *Recent American Fiction: Some Critical Views*, ed. Joseph J. Waldmein, Boston: Houghton Mifflin, 1963.

Lodge, D., *Graham Greene*, New York: Columbia Press, 1966.
—, *The Novelist at the Crossroads*, Ithaca and London: Cornell University Press, 1971.
Lubbock, P., *The Craft of Fiction*, London: Jonathan Cape, 1923.
Lukacs, G., *The Meaning of Contemporary Realism*, trans. John and Necke Mander, London: Merlin Press, 1963.
Macquarrie, J., *An Existentialist Theology: A Comparison of Heidegger and Bultman*, New York: Harper and Row, 1960.
—, *Existentialism*, New York: World Publishing Co., 1972, Penguin Books, 1977.
Marcel, G., *Being and Having: An Existential Diary*, trans. K. Farrer, New York: Harper and Brothers, 1949.
—, *Metaphysical Journal*, trans. Bernard Wall, Chicago: Henry Regnery Co., 1952.
Markovic, V.E,, *The Changing Face: Disintegration of Personality in the Twentieth Century British Novel*, Illinois: Southern Illinois University Press, 1971.
Martin, Graham, *The Modern Age*, ed. Boris Ford, London: Penguin Books, 1961.
Mesnet, Marie-Beatrice, *Graham Greene and The Heart of the Matter*, London: The Cresset Press, 1954.
Muller, W.R., *The Prophetic Voice in Modern Fiction*, New York: Association Press, 1959.
Murry, Krieger, *The Tragic Vision*, New York: Holt Rinehard and Winston, 1960.
Nietzsche, F., *Thus Spake Zarathustra*. trans. A. Tille, New York: Dutton, 1933.
O'Brien, Conor Cruise, *Maria Cross: Imaginative Pattern in a Group of Modern Catholic Writers*, London: Burnes and Oates, 1959.
O'Faolain, Sean, *The Vanishing Hero*, London: Eyre and Spottis Woode, 1956.
Pascal, B., *Pensees*, trans. N.E., Trotter, New York: Dutton, 1958.
Paul, Leslie, *The Meaning of Human Existence*, London: Faber and Faber Ltd., 1949.
Pryce-Jones, David, *Graham Greene*, London: Oliver and Boyd, 1963.
Quennell, Peter, *The Sign of Fish*, London: Collins, 1960.
Reed, H., *The Novel Since 1939*, London, 1947.
Reinhardt, K.F., *The Theological Novel of Modern Europe*, New York, 1969.
Rintelen, Fritz. J. Von, *Beyond Existentialism*, New York, 1962.

Roberts, D.E., *Existentialism and Religious Belief*, New York: O.U.P., 1957.

Rodway Allen, *The Truth of Fiction*, London: Chatto Windus, 1970.

Rollo and May etc., *Existence*, New York: Basic Books, 1958.

Roubiczek, P., *Existentialism: For and Against*, Cambridge, 1964.

Routolo, Lucio P., *Six Existential Heroes*, Massachusetts: Harvard University Press, 1974.

Ryan, John Sprott, *Gleanings from Greeneland*, University of New England, 1972.

Sartre, J.P., *Being and Nothingness: A Phenomenological Essay on Ontology*, trans. Hazel E. Barnes, New York: Philosophical Library, 1956, New York: Washington Square Press, 1975.

—, *Existentialism and Humanism*, trans. Philip Mairet, London, 1948.

—, *Nausea*, trans. Robert Baldick, Penguin Books, 1976.

—, *The Age of Reason*, trans. Eric Sutton, London: Hamish Hamilton, 1947, Penguin Books, 1970.

—, *The Reprieve*, trans. Eric Sutton, London: Hamish Hamilton, 1947, Penguin Books, 1975.

—, *Iron in the Soul*, trans. Gerard Hopkins, London: Hamish Hamilton, 1950, Penguin Books, 1975.

—, *No Exit and Three Other Plays*, trans. Stuart Gilbert, New York, Vintage Books, 1955.

Scholes, R., and Robert, Kellogg, *The Nature of Narrative*, New York: O.U.P., 1966.

Scott, N.A., *Craters of the Spirit: Studies in the Modern Novel*, New York, 1969.

Stratford, P., *Faith and Fiction: Creative Process in Greene and Mauriac*, Notre Dame, 1964.

Tillich, Paul, *The Courage to Be*, New Haven: Yale University Press, 1952.

—, *Biblical Religion and The Search for Ultimate Reality*, Chicago: The University of Chicago Press, 1955.

Trilling, Lionel, *The Opposing Self*, New York: Viking Press, 1955.

Troisfontaines, R., *Existentialism and Christian Thought*, London: 1950.

Vann, J. Don, *Graham Greene: A Checklist*, Kent University Press, 1970.

Wahl, Jean, *A Short History of Existentialism*, trans. Forrest Williams and Stanley Marson, New York: Philosophical Library, 1949.

Warnock, Mary, *Existentialism*, London: O.U.P., 1970.

—, *The Philosophy of Sartre*, London: Hutchinson University Library, 19 5.

West, Morris, *The Devil's Advocate*, New York: Dell Publishing Co., 1959.

West, Paul, *The Modern Novel*, London: Hutchinson and Co., 1963.

—, *Wine of Absurdity*, University Park Pa, 1966.

Wilson, Colin, *The Strength to Dream*, London: Victor Gollancy, 1962.

—, *Beyond the Outsider*, London: Pan Books, 1965.

—, *The Outsider*, London: Pan Books, 1971.

Wolfe, Peter, *Graham Greene the Entertainer*, Illinois: Southern Illinois University Press, 1972.

Wyndham, F., *Graham Greene*, British Council Pamphlet, 1958.

Zabel, M.D., *Craft and Character*, New York: Viking Press, 1957.

(B) Periodicals

1. Articles

Alves, Leonard, "The Relevance of Graham Greene", *English Literature and Language*, 11, 1974.

Arya, J., "Face to Face" (an interview), *Illustrated Weekly of India*, January 19, 1964.

Auden, W.H., "The Heresy of Our Time", *Renascence*, Spring 1949.

Barratt, H., "Adultery as Betrayal in Graham Greene", *Dalhousie Review*, 45, 1965.

Beebe, M., "Criticism of Greene" (a selected checklist), *Modern Fiction Studies*, 3, 3, 1957.

Boardman, G.R., "Greene's Under the Garden: Aesthetic Exploration", *Renascence*, 17, 1965.

Braybroke, N., "Graham Greene: the Double Man: An Approach to *The End of the Affair*", *Queene's Quarterly*, 77, 1952.

Browne, E.M., "Graham Greene: Theatre's Gain", *Theatre Arts*, 45, November, 1961.

Cassidy, J., "America and Innocence: Henry James and Graham Greene", *Blackfriars*, 38, 1957.

Cheney, L., "Joseph Conrad's *The Secret Agent* and Graham Greene's *It's a Battlefield*: A Study in Structural Meaning", *Modern Fiction Studies*, 16, 1970.

Cottrell, B.W., "Second Time Charm: The Theatre of Greene", *Modern Fiction Studies*, 3, 3, 1957.

Day-Lewis, S., "The Dominant Shades of Greene", *Daily Telegraph*, September 15, 1975.

DeVitis, A.A., "Allegory in *Brighton Rock*", *Modern Fiction Studies*, 3, 3, 1957.

Dombrowski, Theo Q., "Graham Greene: Techniques of Intensity", *ARIEL*, 6, 1975.

Downing, F., "Greene and the Case for Disloyalty", *Commonweal*, March 14, 1952.

Donghue, D., "Visit to Greenland", *Commonweal*, November 30, 1973.

Duffy, J.M., "The Lost World of Graham Greene", *Thought*, 33, 1958.

Dunlevy, M., "He could not Win at Russian Roullette", *Canberra Times*, 14, September 25, 1971.

Duran, L., "The Hint of an Explanation of Graham Greene", *Contemporary Review*, 226, March 1975.

Elistratova, A., "Graham Greene and His New Novel", *Soviet Literature*, 8, 1956.

Ellis, W.D., "The Grand Theme of Graham Greene", *Southwest Review*, 41, 1956.

Enerson, G., "Graham Greene", *por Roll Stone*, March 9, 1978.

Evans, R.O., "Existentialism in Graham Greene's *The Quiet American*", *Modern Fiction Studies*, 3, 3, 1957.

Falkner, Peter, "Values in the Novel", *Question*, December, 1975.

Fielding, G., "Graham Greene: the Religious Englishman", *The Listener*, September 24, 1964.

Findlater, R., "Graham Greene as Dramatist", *Twentieth Century*, No., 916, CLIII, 1953.

Grubbs, H., "Albert Camus and Graham Greene", *Modern Language Quarterly*, 10, 1949.

Hegedus, Adam De., "Graham Greene: the Man and his Work", *World Review*, August 1948.

Heilpern, J., "On the Dangerous Edge", *Observer Magazine*, December 7, 1975.

Highet, G., "Our Man in Purgatory", *Horizon*, 3, 1961.

Hinchliffe, A.P., "The Good American", *Twentieth Century*, 168, 1960.

Hoggart, R., "The Force of Caricature", *Essays in Criticism*", 3, 1953.

Hortmann, W., "Graham Greene: The Burnt-Out Catholic", *Twentieth Century Literature*, 10, 1964.

Huber, H.R., "The Two Worlds of Greene", *Modern Fiction Studies*, 3, 3, 1957.

Hynes, J., "The Facts at *The Heart of the Matter*, *Texas Studies in Literature and Language*, 13, Winter, 1972.

Jones, R., "The Human Factor", *The Virginia Quarterly Review*, No. 2, 55, Spring 1979.

Kermode, F., "Mr. Greene's Eggs and Crosses", *Encounter*, 16, 1961.
King, J., "In the Lost Boyhood of Judas: Greene's Early Novels of Hell," *Dalhousie Review*, 49, 1969.
Less, F.N., "Greene: A Comment", *Scrutiny*, 1952.
Lerner, L., "Graham Greene", *Critical Quarterly*, 15, 1963.
Lewis, R.W.B., "The Triology of Greene", *Modern Fiction Studies*, 3, 3, 1957.
—, "The Fiction of Graham Greene: Between the Horror and the Glory", *The Kenyon Review*, XIX, Winter 1957.
Marian, I.H.M., "Graham Greene's People: Being and Becoming", *Renascence*, 18, 1965.
Markovic, V.E., "Graham Greene in Search of God", *Texas Studies in Literature and Language*, V, 1963.
McCall, D., "*Brighton Rock*: The Price of Order", *English Language Notes*, 3, 1966.
McCan, J., "Graham Greene: the Ambiguity of Death", *Por Chr Cent*, April 30, 1975.
Mewshaw, Michael, "Greene in Antibes" (interview), *London Magazine*, No. 2, June-July 17, 1977.
Muller, Charles, H., "Graham Greene and the Absurd", *Unisa English Studies*, No. 2, 10, 1972.
—, "Graham Greene and the Justification of God's Ways", *Unisa English Studies*, No. 1, 10, 1972.
Noxon, J., "Kierkegaard's Stages and *A Burnt-out Case*", *Review of English Literature*, 3, 1962.
O'Faolain, S., "The Novels of Graham Greene", *Britain Today*, No, 148, August 1948.
Patten, K., "The Structure of *The Power and the Glory*", *Modern Fiction Studies*, 3, 3, 1957.
Paul, Leslie, "The Writer and the Human Condition", *The Kenyon Review*, No. 2, XXIX, January 1967.
Peters, W., "The Concern of Graham Greene", *Month*, No. 2, 10, 1953.
Phillips, G.D., "Graham Greene on the Screen", *The Catholic World*, August 1969.
—, "Graham Greene" (an interview), *Twentieth Century*, 25, Summer 1970.
Prichett, V.S., "The World of Graham Greene", *New Statesman*, No. 1399, LV, January 4, 1958.

—, "Human Factor in Graham Greene", *New York Times Magazine*, February 26, 1978.

Rahv, P., "Wicked American Innocence", *Commentary*, 21, 1956.

Rewak, J., "*The Potting Shed*: Maturation of Graham Greene's Vision", *The Catholic World*, 186, 1957.

Rolo, Charles, J., "Graham Greene: the Man and the Message", *Atlantic*, No. 5, 207, May 1961.

Ruotolo, L.P., "*Brighton Rock's* Absurd Heroine", *Modern Language Quarterly*, 25, 1964.

Sackville, W., "The Problem of Despair", *The New Statesman and Nation*, June 1948.

—, "Time-Bomb", *Month*, 25, 1961.

Savage, D.S., "Graham Greene and Belief", *Dalhousie Review*, No. 2, 58, Summer 1978.

Seward, B., "Graham Greene: A Hint of an Explanation", *Western Review*, 22, 1958.

Shorter, E., "Greene: Complaisant Lover", *Drama*, No. 133, Summer 1979.

Smith, A.J.M., "Graham Greene's Theological Thrillers, *Queene's Quarterly*, 68, 1961.

Spier, U., "Melodrama in Graham Greene's *The End of the Affair*, *Modern Fiction Studies*, 3, 3. 1957.

Strange, R., "Graham Greene: The Writer", *New Blackfriars*, 54, January 1973.

Stratford, Philip, "The Uncomplaisant Dramatist: Some Aspects of Graham Greene's Theatre," *Contemporary Literature*, 2, 1961.

—, "Greene's Hall of Mirrors", *The Kenyon Review*, XXIII, Summer 1961.

—, "Unlocking the *Potting Shed*", *The Kenyon Review*, XXIV, 1962.

Taylor, M.A. and Clark, J., "Further Sources for the Second Death by Greene", *Papers on English Language and Literature*, 1, 1965.

Toynbee, Philip, "The Writer's Job" (an interview), *The Hindustan Times*: *Sunday Magazine*, September 29, 1957.

Traversi, D., "Graham Greene", *Twentieth Century*, 149, 1951.

Trilling, D. and Rahv, P., "America and *The Quiet American*", *Commentary*, 22, 1956.

Unsigned Article, "The Greeneland Aboriginal", *New Statesman*, January 13, 1961.

Voorhees, R. J., "The World of Greene", *South Atlantic Quarterly*, 50, 1951.

—, "Recent Greene", *South Atlantic Quarterly*, 62, 1963.

Waugh, E., "Felix Culpa?" *Tablet*, V, June 1948.

Wichert, R.A., "The Quality of Graham Greene's Mercy", *College English*, 25, 1963.

Wilson, A., "The Sense of Evil in the English Novel", *The Kenyon Review*, No. 2, XXIX, Spring 1967.

Woodcook, George, "A Review Article", *Queene's Quarterly*, No. 2, 85, Summer 1978.

2. Reviews

The Man Within: *Times Literary Supplement* (*TLS*)*, June 20, 1929, and *The Bookman*, July 29, 1929.

The Name of Action: *TLS*, October 9, 1930.

Rumour at Nightfall: *TLS*, December 3, 1931.

Stamboul Train: *TLS*, December 15, 1932.

It's a Battlefield: *TLS*, February 8, 1934; *Spectator*, February 9, 1934, and *Life and Letter*, April, 1934.

England Made Me: *TLS*, July 4, 1935; *The New Statesman and Nation*, June 29, 1935, and *The Listener*, July 10, 1935.

A Gun for Sale: *TLS*, July 11, 1936 and *Saturday Review*, June 27, 1936.

Brighton Rock: *TLS*, July 16, 1938; *Saturday Review*, June 25, 1938; *Spectator*, July 15, 1938, and *The London Mercury*, August, 1938.

The Confidential Agent: *TLS*, September 23, 1939, and *Spectator*, September 22, 1939.

The Power and the Glory: *TLS*, March 9, 1940; *Saturday Review*, March 30, 1940, and *Spectator*, March 15, 1940.

The Ministry of Fear: *TLS*, May 29, 1943; *Saturday Review*, June 26, 1943, and *Spectator*, May 28, 1943.

The Heart of the Matter: *TLS*, May 29, 1948; *The New Statesman and Nation*, June 19, 1948; *Spectator*, June 4, 1948, and *Saturday Review*, July 10, 1948.

The Third Man and The Fallen Idol: *TLS*, August 4, 1950.

The End of the Affair: *TLS*, September 7, 1951; *Saturday Review*, October 27, 1951, and *Theatre Arts*, December, 1951.

Nineteen Stories: *TLS*, July 26, 1947, and *The New Statesman and Nation*, August 9, 1947.

Loser Takes All: *TLS*, February 18, 1955, and *The Listener*, February 17, 1955.

The Quiet American: *TLS*, December 9, 1955; *Spectator*, December 9, 1955; *Saturday Review*, March 10, 1956; *The Listener*, December 22, 1955; *Time*, March 12, 1956, and *The New Statesman and Nation*, December 10, 1955.

Our Man in Havana: *TLS*, October 10, 1958; *Spectator*, October 10, 1958; *The Manchester Guardian Weekly*, October 23, 1958, and *Time*, October 27, 1958.

A Burnt-out Case: *TLS*, January 20, 1961; *Spectator*, January 20, 1961; *The Listener*, February 2, 1961, and *Saturday Review*, February 18, 1961.

A Sense of Reality: *Saturday Review*, June 22, 1963 and *The Listener*, June 20, 1963.

Collected Stories: *TLS*, October 20, 1972.

The Comedians: *TLS*, Jannary 27, 1966; *New Statesman*, January 28, 1966; *The Manchester Guardian Weekly*, February 3, 1966; *Spectator*, January 28, 1966; *The Listener*, February 3, 1966, and *The London Magazine*, March, 1966.

The Lost Childhood and Other Essays, *The New Statesman and Nation*, April 15, 1951, and *TLS*, April 6, 1951.

A Sort of Life: *TLS*, September 17, 1971; *Saturday Review*, September 25, 1971, and *New Statesman*, September 17, 1971.

The Honorary Consul: *TLS*, September 14, 1973; *New Statesman*, September 14, 1973; *The Hudson Review*, No. 4, XXIV, Winter 1972-74; *Sewance Review*, No. 1, 82, Winter 1974, and *Encounter*, December 1973.

The Human Factor: *TLS*, March 17, 1978; *New Statesman*, March 17, 1978; *The Listener*, March 16, 1978; *Time*, March 10, 1978; *Spectator*, March 18, 1978; *Sunday Times*, March 5, 1978; *Commonweal*, April 28, 1978; *Sewance Review*, Spring 1978; *Queene's Quarterly*, No. 4, 85, Winter 1978; *Etudes Anglaises*, No. 1, 32, January-March, 1979, and *The Times of India*: *Sunday Magazine*, April 1, 1979.

* *TLS* stands for Times Literary Supplement.

Index

abagado, 90
absurd, 86-7, 109, 141-42
absurdity, 72, 84, 87
absurd man, 84
agage, 142
agape, 34
Allen, Walter, 81
—*Tradition and Dream*, 101
anguish, 72, 78, 135, 139
Atkins, John, 10, 17
Beckett, Samuel, 49, 70, 97
—*Murphy*, 70
—*Waiting for Godot*, 97
Bhagvadgita, 34, 63
Sthita Pragna, 34, 63
Bible, 70
boredom, 115-16, 132, 135
Buber, Martin, preface, 31, 34, 66, 143
—*I-Thou*, 34, 66
—*Pointing the Way*, 66
Camus, Albert, 20, 27, 60, 62, 81, 89, 106-07
—*The Fall*, 81, 101, 107
—*Myth of Sisyphus*, 29, 70, 102
—*The Outsider*, 27, 106
—*The Plague*, 51, 60, 62, 71, 89, 103
philosophical suicide, 20
—*The Rebel*, 28-9
Catholic Herold, The, 6
Christianity, 33, 40, 130
churchless, 40
Comedy, 87-9
Communism, 76, 80, 82, 85-6
Conrad, Joseph, 7, 17, 28, 48, 61, 78, 82, 84, 96, 98
—*The Heart of Darkness*, 96, 129
—*Jim*, 48, 61, 68, 70
—*The Secret Agent*, 17, 28
—*The Victim*, 78, 101
—*Under Western Eyes*, 82, 96, 104
death, 76, 81, 105-08, 122-23
despair, 31-2, 49, 108-10, 125-26
DeVitis, A.A., 29
Dostoyevsky, Fyodor, 40, 57, 65, 67-8, 71, 73, 82, 100, 129
—*The Brothers Karamazov I*, 40, 67-8, 71, 129
—*The Brothers Karamazov II*, 75, 100
—*Notes From the Underground*, 101
dream, 116
engagé dégagé, 86
Essays and Criticism, 100
essence, 72, 80
existence, 72, 80
existentialism, preface, Christian, 14, 30-7, 40, 56
existentialist, 63-4
Atheistic, preface, 32, 72-4
faith, 20, 32, 34-5, 112-14, 141-42
freedom, 78
existential, 86, 111-12, 135, 142-43
Greene, Graham, *Brighton Rock*,

2, 7, 35-41, 46, 63-4, 67, 98, 109, 123, 141
A Burnt-out Case, 56, 58-63, 70-1, 91, 113, 117, 127
—*Collected Essays*, 140-41
—*Carving a Statue*, 128, 134-36
—*The Comedians*, 80, 98, 101-02, 104, 106
—*Complaisant Lover*, 131-34, 136
—*Collected Short Stories*, 105-19
—*England Made Me*, 2, 22-7, 47, 75, 109, 135
—*The End of the Affair*, 7, 45, 52-8, 64, 69, 70, 101-109, 113, 129, 141, 143
—*The Heart of the Matter*, 6-7, 45-52, 54, 64, 68-9, 109, 123, 126, 141
—*The Honorary Consul*, 82, 86-91, 102-03, 106, 108, 141
—*The Human Factor*, 91-7, 103-04, 143
—*In Search of a Character*, 139
—*It's a Battlefield*, 15-22, 24, 26, 28
—*Journey Without Maps*, 7, 10
—*The Living Room*, 6-7, 122-26, 130-32, 136, 141
—*The Lawless Roads*, 102, 142
—*The Man Within*, 2, 6, 12-5, 26, 28, 41, 98, 106, 117, 127, 135
—*The Ministry of Fear*, 50-1
—*The Potting Shed*, 1, 7, 115, 126-31, 134-36, 141
—*The Power and the Glory*, 7, 21, 41-7, 49, 54, 63-4, 68, 90-1, 93, 129, 131-32, 141
—*The Quiet American*, 74-80, 82-3, 86, 88, 100-01, 127
—*Sense of Reality*, 141
—*Stamboul Train*, 6
Short Stories
—The End of the Party, 105-06
—The Second Death, 106-07
—A Chance for Mr Lever, 108-09
—A Drive in the Country, 108-10
—The Basement Room, 110-12, 135
—The Hint of an Explanation, 112
—A Visit to Morin, 114
—Under the Garden, 114-16
—Dream of Strange Land, 116-17
—"I Spy", 117
—Proof Positive, 117
—A Day Saved, 118
—Brother, 118
—The Innocent, 118
—Across the Bridge, 118
—The Case for the Defence, 118
—Men at Work, 118
Hardy, Thomas,
—*Father Time*, 43
Hassan, Ihab, 102
Heideger, Johann Heinrich, 19, 30, 36, 58, 72, 92, 105, 107
—*Dasein*, 36, 72, 92, 105
—*Dasman*, 19, 30, 58, 94, 107
Hindustan Times: Sunday Magazine, 69
Huxley, Aldous, 4-5
Interlinkage, 32
James, Henry, 5
Jaspers, Karl, 7, 30, 35, 66

—*Man in the Modern Age*, 30, 32, 66
—*The Origin and Goal of History*, 66
—*Philosophies*, 67
Jeanson, Francis, 102
Kafka, Franz, 27, 98, 111
—*The Castle*, 27, 111
—*The Trial*, 98, 104
Kaufmann, Walter,
—*Existentialism From Dostoyevsky to Sartre*, 64
Kenyon Review, 71, 100
Kingslake,
—*Eothen*, 16
Kierkegaard, Soren, preface, 7-10, 30-2, 39, 49-52, 56, 62, 66, 72, 115, 126, 133, 143
—*Attack Upon Christendom*, 35, 66
Either/Or, 33, 133
—*Fear and Trembling*, 36
—*The Concluding Unscientific Postscript*, 11, 33, 66
—Leap, 33-4
—Sickness Unto Death, 31, 66
Lerner, Lawrence, 77, 100
Lewis, R.W.B., 100
Life, 75
Lodge, David, 84, 101
London Sunday Times, 75
machismo, 87
Mannheim, Karl
—*Diagnosis of Our Time*, 69
Marcel, Gabriel, 30, 34, 59, 61, 66, 110, 143
—*Being and Having*, 69, 110
—homo-viator, 30-1, 66
—*Metaphysical Journal*, 34, 54, 66, 69
—*The Philosophy of Existence*, 32, 66
marriage, Christian, 132-34
Marxism, 73-4, 95-6
mass existence, 30
Noxon, James, 70
Nottingham Journal, 5
nausea, 72
Outsider, 84
Paul, Leslie, 28, 65
per se, 82
praxis, 74, 80, 85, 90, 98
priori, 84
Prometheus, 41, 116-17
Queene's Quarterly, 103
Rebel, 84
rational and irrational, 86, 140
resentiment, 91
Review of English Literature, 70
Role of the West, The, 77
Rubinoff, Lionel, 103
Russian Roullette, 4
Sartre, Jean-Paul, 4-6, 27, 72-8, 82, 89, 91, 96-7, 111, 143
—*The Age of Reason*, 89, 97, 103
—*Being and Nothingness*, 74, 100-01
—for-itself, 72, 76, 94
—in-itself, 94
—Being for-others, 72, 118
—*Iron in the Soul*, 77, 100
—interiorization, 96
—*Existentialism and Humanism*, 100, 103-04
—*The Problem of Method*, 100
—*Nausea*, 100-01
—*Roads to Freedom*, 111
—Roquentin, 82
—mauvaise foi, 78, 101
—Third man, look, 74
—us-object experience, 80
—Third force, 79-80

Sisyphus, 118-19
Tillich, Paul, 32, 34, 64, 143
—*The Courage to Be*, 32, 34
—*Dynamics of Faith*, 67
Times, The, 5, 6, 8
Tolstoy, Leo, Karenin, 61, 130
Uncle Remus, 96
Victim, 84
Wilson, Colin, 4, 15, 28, 128, 135
—*Beyond the Outsider*, 28
—indifference threshold, St. Neot Margin, 4, 15, 128, 135
Yale French Studies, 102

PR 6013 .R44 R3 1983
Rai, Gangeshwar
Graham Greene: an existential approach